So long,
So far away
Is Africa.
Not even memories alive
Save those that history books create,
Save those that songs
Beat back into the blood—
Beat out of blood with words sad-sung
In strange un-Negro tongue
So long,
So far away
Is Africa.

Subdued and time-lost
Are the drums—and yet
Through some vast mist of race
There comes this song
I do not understand,
This song of atavistic land,
Of bitter yearnings lost.

Without a place—
So long,
So far away
Is Africa's
Dark face.

I want to teach my sons how
    To live this life on earth,
To face its struggles and its strife,
    And to improve their worth.
    Not just the lesson in a book
        Or how the rivers flow,
But how to choose the proper path
    Wherever they may go,
    To understand eternal truth
    And know the right from wrong
And gather all the beauty of a flower
    and a song; For if
I help the world to grow in wisdom
        and grace,
Then I shall feel that I have won
    And I have helped my race.
And so I ask Your guidance, God,
    That I may do my part
    For character and confidence
    And happiness of heart.

                    Your dad,
                    Harvey Alston

BLACK MALES

*An African American View
on Raising Young Men*

Harvey Alston Best, Inc.

KENDALL/HUNT PUBLISHING COMPANY
4050 Westmark Drive Dubuque, Iowa 52002

Little Eyes Upon You
Author Unknown

There are little eyes upon you
  and they're watching night and day.
There are little ears that quickly
  take in every word you say.
There are little hands all eager
  to do anything you do;
And a little man who's dreaming
  of the day he'll be like you.

You're the little fellow's idol,
  you're the wisest of the wise.
In his little mind about you
  no suspicions ever rise.
He believes in you devoutly,
  holds all that you say and do;
He will say and do, in your way,
  when he's grown up like you.

There's a wide eyed little fellow
  who believes you're always right;
And his eyes are always opened,
  and he watched day and night.
You are setting an example
  every day in all you do.
For the little man who's waiting
  to grow up to be like you.

Contents

▦ CHAPTER 15: Self-Esteem, 143

Foreword

African Americans are victims of a never ending internal war. Like survivors of all of the wars, we who are still alive are veterans. Not veterans of foreign wars, but veterans of homeland racism; veterans of cruel and unjust slavery; veterans of years of segregation, and veterans of desegregation, and all kinds of other types of forced inhumanities because of our race.

American prisoners of war were sometimes psychologically brainwashed and the result was to take on the "cause" of the captors. Our armed services developed a system of de-programming; a system of re-orientation back to the American values. Upon safe arrival in America, many of the POWs were dysfunctional. Their family life was no longer a place filled with love and care, but was like one more battleground. To kill the inner pain many POWs turned to alcohol or drugs, leaving many mentally scarred and physically torn. Flashbacks brought nightmares into the daytime. With the lack of job opportunity the internal pressure continued to build.

African American slaves (prisoners of race) were psychologically brainwashed resulting in a perceived inferiority complex that came not from two long years of imprisonment, but from a process exceeding one hundred years. Many African Americans similar to POWs took up the cause of their captors because there was no system for re-programming or re-orientation back to African heritage values.

Our POW's of slavery were separated from their families. They had no form of community love or fellowship to help and ease the pain. In the daytime their lives were filled with nightmares and hate.

Today, one out of every four African American young men between the ages of twenty and twenty-nine are either in jail, on trial, or on parole. The leading cause of death among

African American young men is murder, and murder by the hands of other African American young men.

As a nation we are losing our Black males. We are losing them mentally, emotionally, economically, and through death.

This book was written to offer suggestions to parents who may lack the information to motivate their son. Now more than ever there is a deep and profound National need for African American parents to unite together for the sake of our children. To collectively raise them, educate and equip them, to live in harmony with one another, free of the prejudices and bigotry which have divided our Nation for decades. This book *Black Males: An African American View on Raising Young Men*, is about pride, heritage, integrity and celebration. I use the humor of real life and a philosophy of active parenting to instill into the next generation of Black Males, a sense of National Identity.

Dedicated to Fannie Mary Merriweather Alston

Fannie grew up in a large family. When she was a sophomore in college, her father had a stroke that incapacitated him. Her mother reared seven children with the primary emphasis placed on their education. As soon as the older children finished four years of college, they were expected to get a job and help the younger ones. Fannie entered school (first grade) at age five. She finished high school and entered college at Alabama A & M at age seventeen. She received a B.S. degree in Home Economics and was qualified to teach elementary grades one through eight. She received a M.Ed. degree with reading certification in graduate school. Unable to find work in the Columbus School System because Champion Avenue School was the only school in Columbus where an African American could teach Home Economics in 1944, and the position was already filled, she was told by the superintendent to pick up a few elementary courses so she could get a job in Urban Crest.

Needing a job immediately, she worked at Curtiss Wright and North American aircraft plant. After seven and one-half years she was laid off. It was at this time she went back to school for retraining in Elementary Education.

Fannie then proceeded to teach fourt and fifth grades, and reading, in the Columbus Public Schools for twenty eight and one-half years.

She is a charter member of The Good Shepherd Baptist Church, The National Sorority of Phi Delta Kappa, Gamma Alpha Chapter, and a member of Top Ladies of Distinction, Inc.

She was married forty years to Harvey H. Alston, Sr., now deceased. She is now the mother of two children and five grandchildren.

In 1983 at 8 A.M., she stopped at the drive-through of the Huntington Bank located on High Street—in route to her job at Second Avenue—just a couple of blocks south of High Street. A robber approached her vehicle and demanded that she open the door. She refused. At this time the robber shot through the window, the bullet striking her in the hip where it is still lodged.

She retired from the Columbus School System in 1987. One and one-half years before she planned, because her mother could no longer be left alone. Since 1987, she has traveled to Tuscaloosa Alabama every three to four months, alternating as caregiver for her mother who is now over one hundred years old. She attributes her mother's longevity to the fact that she is able to stay in her own home, among familiar surroundings.

Acknowledgments

When I start to say "thanks" to the ones who have helped me in so many ways, I am reminded of the story of the many who were cleansed of leprosy and only one returned to say "thanks." I am trying to be the one who says "thanks."

To my wife Toni and my two sons, Paul and William, without your love I am nothing.

To my mother, whose strong religious faith in God, and constant prayers have kept His light shining on me. For this I am truly blessed.

To my staff, who stand by me always, even though we may have bitten off more than we could chew.

To "Doc," Dr. Charles Flowers, for his constant counsel and for being my hero.

To my best friend Bill Rose, who sets new goals for me by challenging and setting the pace so that I have someone to catch up with.

To Reverend and Mrs. Nelson Crawley for standing by me, and for their support as my family. Sarah and Nelson are also my aunt and uncle.

To Robert Wright, who finds a book a month for me to read. Robert is more than an employee, he is part of our family.

To the African American students and staff at the schools where I have spoken. You are my inspiration. Your love and appreciation for my work gives me the courage to continue. Your letters also brighten my day and lift my heart.

To my audiences everywhere—without you—there is no me.

To all whose path has met mine, whose lives, if for only a moment, touched mine. For what life has given me, and the opportunity to have known you I am eternally grateful.

Introduction

Africa covers 11,700,000 square miles—or one-fifth of the entire land area of the world. The United States would fit into Africa more than three times. Archaeologists have found evidence of humans who lived in Africa about 4.5 million years ago. Today, Africa has about six hundred million people. At least eight hundred African languages and dialects are spoken in the nation. Of all the kingdoms and empires of early African, ancient Egypt made the greatest impression. Kunta Kinte was one of the estimated fifty million black Africans who became victims of the slave trade. Europeans quickly found several ways to obtain African slaves. The most common method was to turn one group of Africans against another. They offered foreign aid, (guns and liquor) to an African ruler in exchange for slaves. (Guns and drugs still remain our greatest source of destruction.) It would take nearly two hundred fifty years of enslavement before it would end. At the end of slavery, came the start of segregation. Separate black churches and schools started because, we could not pray to God in white churches or educate our children in white schools.

Our struggle for freedom is still just a dream. We still have to fight for equal rights. We are still discriminated against, laws are enforced against poor black and not against rich whites. Our children are not provided with an equal education. The aftermath of slavery, segregation, and racism, have left deep scars on our African American young men and they are still struggling for survival.

▐ CHAPTER 1
Up Hill Climb

"If there is no struggle, there is no progress."
—Frederick Douglass

I only want you to win with your African American young men. But you must understand that the winning path is less traveled. I want to offer you an opportunity to do something remarkable with your son. Consider all the ideas I will present with the hope that we as a nation might win with our men.

I know you are smart, but for the lack of time you don't have the opportunity to become familiar with all of the new child-rearing ideas. To even pick up a book like this suggests three things about you: *First*, you have an African American young man or have one somewhere in your life. You're curious about what this book has to offer, and intrigued by the prospect of a unique, helpful and fresh approach. *Second*: you are.....puzzled about why so many African American young men drop out of school, go to jail, or end up dead. *Third*, you are looking for the solutions to so many problems.

Don't put this book down without considering the risks! You hold in your hand the blueprint for creating the next generation of African American men. There aren't many around, and this book is strictly for changing ordinary young men into extraordinary African Americans. Men who can move mountains and with a focused purpose, can change the world.

Our African American Young Men Are in Danger

There are powerful and sinister forces operating in our world right now. They are white, bold and stealthy, and intent on wrestling greatness from the grasp of our African American young men. These forces are not always obvious or easy to spot. Collectively we can learn how to spot them and beat them at their own game. We can create a generation of African American young men that represent our greatest national achievement. As they said in the south, "we can hang together, or we can hang alone."

I am a hopeless optimist. I have seen the enemy of this struggle and I believe that this victory can be had! This book offers part of the solution. I take the mission to save our

African American young men very seriously. In the midst of raising Black males in a world intent on neutralizing them, we can find complete victory and the inner joy that follows doing something good for the world.

I thoroughly expect that certain parts of this book will rattle your thinking. That's good. The rattling on the cage might be annoying, yet I promise you that working through these ideas will yield terrific value.

History is filled with examples of "victory at hand," that were only to be lost due to negligence or stubbornness of leadership. I believe that Sickle cell anemia should have been cured years ago, and that equal rights for all of God's children should have been won by now! I also believe that every game, every deal, every interaction has a crucial moment, a fulcrum, upon which the final outcome swings. Finally, believe that the difference between winning and losing can come down to a small event.

Don't lose your child because you chose to live by your ego, rather than by the possibilities. The stakes are too high. Your African American young man's life is too valuable to ignore any sensible suggestion to make him better.

It's Easier to Build African American Young Men Than to Repair One in Jail

Broken Black men surround us, and are the focus of intense t.v. and newspaper attention. How often have we read about the "Black man," his lack of sensitive and uninformed male leadership in our African American culture and families, and a general absence of strong Black male role models in our society? It makes sense to raise young Black males to be good men, but how, when we are told repeatedly in history that we are a broken and discredited race? That simple statement only hints at the radical nature of the rescue mission, we as parents need to perform. We must swing into immediate action because our African American young men aren't waiting around for us. They are encountering new situations and learning experiences daily, that are shaping both their collective identity and individual destiny. We must move to change the course of events, now!

Mothers Only

Most of the childrearing books are read by women. Your natural role as an African American mother puts you in a unique position. You want your son to grow up to be a good man, but you don't know much about that. You've been a woman your whole life! You are open to ideas about how to raise African American young men, and know that to rear a healthy son requires a team (village) effort where everyone pitches in.

In a perfect, white world, mothers and fathers happily unite in raising their little boys and girls. Each partner contributing unique and vital elements. In the real America, we are all doing the best we can. Our world is often filled with mistakes, fathers that aren't around, or who won't stand up and be counted, and lousy trade-offs between kids, and responsibilities, and our jobs.

I've known many single mom's who are raising young men alone. Saying that it's "difficult" somehow fails to capture all of the trouble involved. I asked a women how her son was doing in school, and she replied, "I don't know, I've got my own problems!"

I don't know what your situation is. I hope your life is satisfying, but it may be far from it. The good news is *whether your situation is* **good** *or* **bad** *doesn't need to have a bearing on how your son eventually turns out.* Plenty of "bad seeds" have sprung from great, unified homes, and many good solid young men have come from unfit homes. With that in mind, take some hope that no matter what your circumstance, single, married, divorced or widowed, you can raise a healthy young man if you *know what to do.*

"What to do" now involves a number of activities. Your contribution as a mother essentially involves four items: 1) Demonstrating your unique maternal love for your African American young man, 2) realizing that what your son sees of you is what he will see of women in general, 3) develop his

"softer" side, and 4) push him out toward masculinity. Let's look at each of these.

Phase I

1) You must actively and freely love your son. It is *the most vital thing* you can do to raise a healthy African American young man. A young man that knows he is loved can suffer massive tragedy and still be alright. But, remember this: It doesn't matter how much you say it is if he "can't hear it." The meaning of "I love you" is how he interprets it. Assume responsibility to make the message clear.

Phase II

2) How your son relates with you creates a beginning point, for young man to relate with young woman in general. You are the ambassador of women to your son. Let him get a good balanced view of what womanhood is all about, and let him create a good solid relationship with you. How?

A lot of talk is out there about the differences between Black men and Black women. A huge gulf still separates mothers and fathers. Mothers, cannot understand the pressures and expectations fathers harbor in their hearts. Fathers, are clearly out of touch with the unique female environment. Mutual understanding between parental forces is difficult to establish, so we must press on in creating the best relationship possible in a sometimes adversarial environment.

3) Develop his "softer" side. One simple idea will help build mutual understanding. Black women are a combination of feminine and masculine traits, and Black men are a combination of masculine and feminine traits. Each of us to some extent or another, share qualities of the opposite sex. How does this relate to African American young men? Help your son appreciate that which is foreign to him: Femaleness. That means intuition, understanding, warmth, emotional depth, perseverance and courage. This book will help you understand how to build these in the most effective way.

4) Lastly, push your son toward masculinity. You might picture raising an African American young man as a "push/pull" arrangement. Due to simple biological survival, a Black males first attachment is to you, his mother. Dad's role is that of support. As time progresses, Dad (or some other male) takes on a new role of pulling this child toward him. As he pulls (assuming that some male does) you must push. Give your son permission, encouragement and support as he makes the vital transition. You know intuitively that this is what you must do, and this book will show you the steps to take.

You are eminently qualified for this job. Some of you are doing the job all alone. I wholeheartedly welcome you, to a great source of insight, that will encourage and help you. If you have to, or want to, you can raise a healthy son alone.

Black males need considerable maternal advice and input to be healthy. Forget those who say Black males are mothered too much these days. That only happens in rare cases. It would be more appropriate to say that Black males are *underfathered*, because that's the glaring problem.

Both Black men and Black women will find this book interesting reading. You may at times be distracted by the Black male spin I apply to ideas, but please don't take offense. My motives are purely to offer an aggressive and interesting approach to raising African American young men.

In African cultures, when young men become teenagers, they get "called out" by the elder tribesman to be trained as "men." Raising a son is of most importance. Whether you are single or married, go to your sons father or significant other, and "call him out!" There's work to be done.

Men Only

I need to talk to you for a moment, Black man to Black man. For most Black males, such a suggestion conjures up an image of trouble. Do yourself a favor and strike such a negative image, for what I am about to tell you is the closest you will ever come to giving life.

This whole parenting circus probably came on you by storm. There is no way to adequately prepare for what happened. First there is pregnancy. Then there is child-birth, the single most unnatural thing to a man that he can ever be involved with! Then there is the first year, when it doesn't seem as though your presence matters to anyone, least of all "your" baby. This is surely an "outside-looking-in" deal.

When do you become important? Well, sometime between bedwetting, and being asked for the keys to the car. To be more specific, you are important and valuable as soon as you *make yourself important and valuable.* Most dad's don't discover this until it's too late. It reminds me of a speaker I heard once who said there are three kinds of dad's: Those that make things happen, those that watch things happen, and those that ask what happened!

Now I won't start nagging you about how lousy dad's are these days. There are other books around that can do that. Interestingly enough, when I sat down to write this book, I knew that the vast majority of Black men in this country don't read childrearing books. I clearly understand why.

The reason Black men don't read child-rearing books is because these books are way too centered on "white" culture. Nothing about these fine books appeal to a Black man, and frankly bores them. Think about how many other Black men you know who have actually sat down and read a child-rearing book. You'll only need one hand to count.

This might be the first, but I hope not the last one you ever read. Let me just say that there are things you can do to become the difference between average and awesome for you son. In the midst of confusing advise, busy schedules, evaporating dreams, drying up like the *Raisin In The Sun* and perhaps a life that is going no place, you'll find this book a formula for success. Your *son's* success.

Would you like a secret formula that would let you win for the African American race? To raise an exceptional son, you need the right fuel.

The formula is a series of ingredients that *don't come to you* from a book like this, but that *come out of you.* Your African American young man needs you. He needs some special things from you. He needs your confirmation, your affirmation, and your motivation. Mix well and serve warm with love.

An African American young man needs your confirmation. That means that African American young men are looking to adult Black males to tell them they are alright. Beginning around the age of five Black young men are attracted to men like little sponges. They just want to know that they are worthy, that they are acceptable, that they measure up in your eyes and that they mean something special to you. It takes so little to confirm them. Tell them that they are the greatest, and back it up with your actions.

African American young men need affirmation. Remember that they barely know "up from down" and they need your direction and support to know how to grow. They will beg for such direction in so many non-verbal ways, and you must be willing to take a stand and speak into their little lives. It's oxygen for them.

African American young men need your motivation. They need your brain, your schemes, your dreams, your push and glow. Give it to them. If you have no idea how to begin, then read on. You have what they want, you just don't know it yet.

The future of our world depends on you raising African American young men of high caliber. Forget about how your mother raised you, or that your dad was not around. Forget about those fringe "Black men problems," that are getting so much unwarranted attention these days. What difference do they make in what actions you choose today? None! Fix your sight on the real problem: Raising African American young men fit to change the world. Raising African American young man that you in your heart know are your finest.

The vast majority of Black males, ninety-four to ninety-eight percent are perfectly normal. Black males need considerable input from both men and women, because they are a blend of both. They are driven to seek the qualities of both sexes, and will search for those attributes whether you provide them or not. Black males are resilient, and will seek out those things they need to grow and answer their questions. You want a way to push your son to the top. To raise them requires the coordinated action of many people. It's a team effort involving unity among not only moms and dads, but others including grandparents, teachers, and community leaders.

⊞ CHAPTER 2
Winners

When you control a man's thinking, you do not have to worry about his actions. You do not have to tell him not to stand here or go yonder. He will find his "proper place" and will stay in it. You do not need to send him to the back door. He will go without being told. In fact, if there is no back door, he will cut one for his special benefit.

—Carter G. Woodson

What Is an African American Young Male?

We're going to create a reasonably sized, workable claim. *African American young men are males between the ages of five and twelve.* Males before this age are what I would call "babies," and for lots of physical and psychological reasons they are so different that we really can't easily include them in this discussion. Young men older than twelve are teenagers, and parents of those young men know they are an entirely different sort of beast.

African American young men are highly explosive. By that I mean that *the average run-of-the-mill five to twelve year old African American young men* have potential far beyond what his parents credit him for. He's destined at birth for a spectacular life. He is an intense focus of energy, an adventurer, a laboratory, a sound studio, a puzzle, a playground, a toy, a source of love, and a one of a kind contribution to the world! The African American young man living in your home today is gifted with at least one attribute that sets him apart from all other young men his age. He is easily capable of changing the world and attaining anything in life that he wants. But the color of his skin makes him a target for others.

You were this way once, too. But life unfolded, forcing you and molding your personality down a path to where you are now. Life's racist experiences, focused and chiseled at your considerable potential at several spots along the way. Doesn't it seem strange how the course of your life would bring you from that open, "anything is possible" potential of birth, to this narrow adult view? Your life was explosive, just like your African American young man's. Will you do more with your son's explosiveness than what was done with yours?

What's a Good Young Black Male?

All Black males are good Black males. Now. . .do me a favor and don't burst out in laughter! I say this not from the position of a blind humanitarian, but from a position that recognizes the total innocence in which God brought children into this world. They are designable and moldable, in an infinite variety of ways. All African American young men devote a good deal of their early lives eagerly collecting information and building basic attitudes and beliefs upon which they will live the rest of life. You play a role in that. Uncountable numbers of factors and forces intermingle in the minds of African American young men during this age. It is within this swirling cauldron of experience that African American young men begin making decisions and living life by their own ability. For better or worse, they make the best decisions they can with the information they have available, and begin the arduous task of learning by experience. They are looking for help, regardless of how tough, independent and carefree they may act on the outside. Parents and caretakers are in a perfect position to build good African American young men if they take the time to understand this process, and appreciate the forces that control his frame of reference.

What's a good African American young man? Let's not get the water too muddied up here. Good sons are simply obedient, sensitive, helpful, conversant, polite, thoughtful; your basic Boy Scout profile. You can depend on them (most of the time) to think clearly, make good decisions, exhibit honesty, be well-rounded, and teachable. These are the qualities of good African American young men.

What motivates an African American young man to act good? What will make these attributes viable and survivable throughout his adulthood? How do we teach sons to begin these traits? The answer to these questions, coil and intertwine to form a rope, with which your son can "lasso" excellence.

The large strands in this rope of goodness seem to be:

A.   A personal urge to live up to some high white standard,
B.   The developing maturity of African American young males
C.   Habits of discipline
D.   A developed sense of love and caring
E.   Bold, exemplary models.

If you read carefully, you will notice that this list is a collection of biological drives, and learned behavior. I don't think biology and learning are the sum of the developmental forces which mold African American young men, but they can provide a clear starting spot to begin our discussion.

African American young males acquire a sensitivity to the moral values of good behavior in church (though it's difficult to pin-point when this spiritual sensitivity is learned). It seems to be a common urge that dominates African American young males. Even though this is by no means a constant motivation, a moral bearing is generally in force in young men.

The force of maturity is of a biological origin. All African American young men do grow up, and through the seasoning process of life develop an appreciation of the benefits of good behavior. Most African American young men learn that those who act in white, socially acceptable ways get rewarded, and those that don't get penalized. Maturity makes this recognition possible.

All African American young men are well disciplined. Think about this: The root of the word "discipline" is the same root as the word "disciple." African American young men that are disciplined have been taught to be disciples of something or someone. They have been given a clear set of standards to live up to, and have been shown how to live according to those standards. Disciplined African American young men are good disciples with good habits. The level of quality that the disciplined African American young male develops into is proportional to the quality of his discipleship.

African American young men are *not* born, to be loving and caring, they are taught. Good African American young men have to be reared to treat others with love and care and act in those ways, due to practice.

African American young men typically have bold, exemplary models by which they can model themselves. From birth until death, we pick and choose aspects of others that we like and admire. The more defined and modelable the behavior of those we admire, the more we are likely to find ourselves conforming to them. This of course is particularly true about sons, who are constantly on the look out for new, distinctive and interesting ways to act. African American young men have to have some kind of good behavior modeled by significant individuals in their life.

What's a Good Black Man?

There are some books and articles around today that don't say very nice things about Black men. Ignore that chatter. Black men for the most part are very nice, and the good ones decisively outnumber the bad ones.

The top ideal Black man as reported by middle school students was a list which included such people as: Martin Luther King, Malcolm X, Booker T. Washington and W.E.B. DuBoise. What made them ideal? Caring and loving was stated first, followed by such qualities as: intelligence, morality/honesty, sensitivity, courage, and family orientation.

Any surprise? No. Though the institution of Black manhood has suffered many attacks over the last decade, consensus on what makes a good Black man is *easy* to find. We assign great value to issues such as: leadership, initiative, courage, good decision-making skills, wisdom and discernment, strength of character, lovingness, kindness, standing for what one thinks is right, integrity, and providing for the family. These are qualities of good Black men.

Though some might argue about the infamous qualities of some of these *men*, I don't expect anyone would argue the profundity of the *qualities*. These qualities are timeless, "adhesive" sorts of traits that unite people of all societies.

I would like to suggest a reasonable definition of a "good black man" is the *behavioral enactment of these qualities.* This definition is wordless; it is the personification of these qualities in real-live Black men. In other words, you can only point out the definition when you see it! Because, such a definition uses no words, we are free of entrapment in vague ideologies about Black men and can unequivocally point out goodness when we see it.

Black men who get labeled "good" often have an "automatic" lifestyle of goodness. They don't just "get good" from time to time, but act in ways that are good on a regular basis.

Good Black men, though not perfect, have habits of good-ness, dependability and an active conscience to match.

We can certainly agree that these qualities and ideals are much easier to write about than to achieve. Talk is cheap, but I'm a true believer. I believe in setting exceptionally high marks, and endeavoring to achieve them. There is always the possibility of failure, but if you don't aim high, you'll only hit the low things. Let's shoot the moon and try to build good Black men!

This poem by Rudyard Kipling consummates in verse both an inspiring definition of a good man, and the intensity of our challenge in building good winners.

"*If* . . ."

If you can keep your head when all about you
　　are losing theirs and blaming it on you,
If you can trust yourself when all men doubt you,
　　But make allowances for their doubting too;
If you can wait and not be tired by waiting,
　　Or being lied about, don't deal in lies,
Or being hated, don't give way to hating,
　　And yet don't look too good, nor talk too wise;
If you can dream—and not make dreams your master;
　　If you can think—and not make thoughts your aim;
If you can meet with Triumph and Disaster
　　and treat those two impostors the same;
If you can bear to hear the truth you've spoken
　　Twisted by knaves to make traps for fools,
Or watch the things you gave your life to, broken,
　　And stoop and build 'em up with worn out tools;
If you can make one heap of all your winnings
　　And risk it on one turn of pitch-and-toss,
And lose, and start again at your beginnings
　　And never breath a word about your loss;
If you can force your heart and nerve and sinew
　　To serve your turn long after they are gone,
And so hold on when there is nothing in you
　　Except the will which says to them: "Hold on!"
If you can talk with crowds and keep your virtue,
　　Or walk with Kings—nor lose the common touch,
If neither foes nor loving friends can hurt you,
　　If all men count with you, but none too much;
If you can fill the unforgiving minute
　　With sixty seconds' worth of distance run,
Yours is the Earth and everything that's in it,
　　And—which is more—you'll be a Man, my son!

▦ CHAPTER 3

How Do We Raise African American Young Men Into Good Black Men?

What happens to a dream deferred? Does it dry up like a raisin in the sun?

—Langston Hughes

What a great question! If the answer to the question were obvious, don't you think everyone would recognize it? Of course they would, but raising a winner is not that obvious. It's a fact that winners have been raised out of every known and conceivable family situation. It's a mystery how delightful winners can rise up from ruinous and low life situations and losers can plunge down from lives of privilege and success. What I am sure about is, that if you want your son to be average, do for him average things. If you would instead choose for his life to be remarkable, your course of action must be equally remarkable.

Let me ask you a thought-provoking question that relates directly with raising a winner: Why did you have kids? Think hard on this because your answer will indicate the extent to which you will pursue your sons explosive potential. Statistics reveal that most pregnancies are accidents. That means that half the children in the world today were *unplanned and possibly unwanted,* some of them were conceived when contraception was in use. How welcomed do you think those little surprises were? Only a few children were both planned and wanted! Ask yourself why you had children. Some of the most common answers are:

> *"I wanted someone to love me"*
> *"I wanted to carry on the family name"*
> *"I wanted the chance to raise a child"*
> *"I wanted companionship when I get old"*

Perhaps you are in the category of those who just had children by accident. You no doubt remember the justification you used to make yourself feel better about that situation!

I want you to notice something: These reasons listed for having children are all *self*-serving reasons. Notice that they have nothing to do with the child personally, but have everything to do with you. Listen carefully to them:

> *"So* I *can have someone to love me,"*
> *"So* I *can carry on the family name,"*
> *"I want to raise a child,"*
> *"I want companionship."*

These reasons are frighteningly self-centered and one-sided.

If your reasons for having a child are selfish, you will raise them *under the direction of your selfish wishes*. Not for their purpose and life, but for yours! *You're not alone*, for the vast majority of parents are raising African American young men under such misconstrued pretenses right now! Though it's too late to give your kid back, or to start over, the situation isn't terminal. What if you want to change? Are there unselfish reasons for wanting a child? There is only one that I know of and you can start to practice it now: Having a child *for the child's sake*. Think about this. If your purpose in having and raising kids is a "child's life for the child's sake," this purpose dictates a vastly different child-rearing formula that those who are raising kids for their purpose.

Now stop and consider what this means. You would certainly not back off and let them develop at will. If you raised your son for his own sake, you would seize every opportunity to build and direct him to become a good Black man and seize *his own destiny*! Such a value would demand immediate action on your part to help your son wring the most out of his own life. How do you do that? That's a million dollar question deserving a million dollar reply.

I suggest eight qualities you must build in him to help your son grow to be a good Black man and conquer his destiny.

Eight Winning Qualities

There are eight (8) buildable qualities that are used to build and form the foundation of winning African American young men:

1. African American young men that can relate with their parents
2. African American young men that can open up and talk about themselves
3. African American young men that can be curious, imaginative and creative

4. African American young men that have good disciplined habits
5. African American young men that have good attitudes
6. African American young men that understand winning and losing through athletics
7. African American young men that have complete mastery over one skill
8. African American young men that have a spiritual foundation

African American young men who are raised to personify these qualities would be remarkable by any standard. Wouldn't you agree? What's important to understand is that at this moment, we have a radiant opportunity to raise up sons with these qualities. Your son can be like this, starting here and starting now!

While we're filled with excitement about this possibility, let me suggest something even more radical. Why don't we attempt to build a generation of Black men that are better than *all of this*. Let's really think big! Using these qualities as our guide, let's create Black men that are tough, resourceful, creative, full of drive and full of care. Hard working winners, capable, faithful powerful black forces in a white world that is working constantly to sidetrack them. Are there names for men like this? Yes. . . African American Men.

What in the World Is an "African American Man?"

The original African American man started in the early 19th century as the world emerged from slavery. It was a remarkable moment in history when brave Black individuals set upon a course to revive traditional elements of goodness and excellence in black men. These "African American men" chose to revive the traditional elements that graced African and Egyptian cultures qualities such as: appreciation for the skills in the arts, music, debate, athletic prowess, inventiveness and creativity. The African American of this moment in time, was searching for the stolen identity.

We face a New African American today. It is an urgent time that is now on us. Technological and social changes are making jobs hard to find, the world is shrinking due to communication and population, confusion is mounting, never seen before world-wide economies are forming, and the search for our role and purpose is taunting our sensibilities. What a great time to be alive and be an African American! What great opportunities exist for those of us who are prepared to recognize and master them!

We need African American men to successfully navigate life into the next century. Answers to the complex combination of problems facing us today have yet to be devised. Where are the answers going to come from? The answers will come from the greatest minds we can offer. The minds of most of the African American men are now being used to do lesser work, and their true genius is being wasted! If there ever is a time that the world needs the Black race to step forward and assume leadership, it is now!

African American men are **made** men. They are made from African American young men, raised with the eight buildable qualities of goodness we've already discussed. Using these qualities as the point of reference, you have the opportunity to build Black men of today. It will take a long "stretch" on your part, but it is well within the grasp of both, you and your son.

Tomorrow and Tomorrow

My obsession is with tomorrow. *African American young men!* Aim at tomorrow, and take us sprinting directly into the future. You must learn to feel this acceleration, and *don't look back*. There's a saying "if you're not the lead dog, then you can smell the shit." The sad truth about the job we have before us is that this world doesn't really care about you or your son. The world doesn't care if you're a leader or a follower, a success or a flop, or anything else. The white world wants to force you into a rut because, from the world's perspective, that's the safest place for you. If you're out of sight, you can't cause any trouble!

You are not a robot, born into this world to thoughtlessly act. You are a unique human being with one quality that is your greatest asset: the initiative to choose. You can be the point man, the team leader, the coach, the captain who is making the choices and calling the shots. You can capitalize on your qualities every time you choose to act. Understand that the people around you are probably waiting to be told what to do. Some people need to be led, and are waiting for a person with a purpose, to step forward.

I am going to suggest many things for you to do to distinguish your purpose. You may do them, or ignore them, it's up to you. It's your requisite choice to use or not to use.

Now, some of you will do these things and others won't. I believe your choice boils down to an issue of love. Do you love your son enough to stretch above and beyond the call of duty and attempt to save his life? No one can predict how much success you might have with this, but I do know that if you don't try, your fate is sealed.

Action to Take: *You must consciously make a choice to help your son sail in the seas of the African American manhood. Sit down with him and tell what you are going to do and why. Tell him that you two are going to take an adventure together that will last a lifetime!*

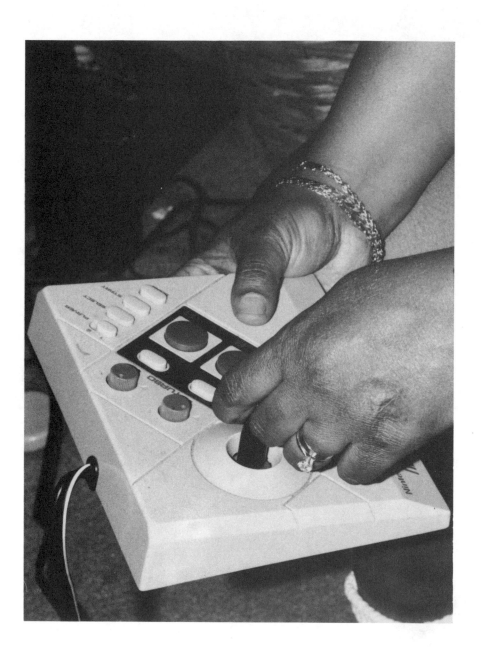

⚏ CHAPTER 4
An Unconventional Approach: The Five Most Common Parenting Screw-ups

The pasts of his ancestors lean against him.
Crowd him. Fog out his identity.

Getting your African American young man from point A to Z, on the road map of life demands that you first figure out where you are. I want to discuss five general patterns of parenting that represent where most parents are. These issues aren't particularly good, so if you're not listed below, don't worry; it may actually be good news! If you do find your location on this list just remember that few things are permanent, least of all a parenting problem! I'll now outline the foul patterns, and offer corrections for them shortly.

The five parenting screw-ups are:

1. All Talk/No Action
2. No Vision/No Plan
3. "Bolts-in-the-Neck" Parenthood
4. The lights are on and no one is home
5. Letting Time Steal Your Life

Screw-up #1: All Talk/No Action

You'll pay a very high price for doing nothing for your son. I'm always flabbergasted at the number of parents I see practicing "hands-off" parenting. They evidently haven't an understanding of the risk. If you don't mind having life steam-roll your son, then I suppose talking big and doing nothing for him is acceptable. But that's not what you want.

I mean something very specific by "doing nothing." You need to ask yourself "How much am I doing compared to what I am *capable of doing?*" You may well have the best "action" intention in the world, yet come up short in performance! This comparison highlights a mental trick we play on ourselves, which is responsible for many of life's problems. In order to remain comfortable with ourselves, we need to believe that we are doing "the best we can do." We become experts not in action, but in persuading ourselves that under the circumstances, we are giving our "best effort." This is usually a flawless "self-con job." It chokes off parental effectiveness by allowing us to think we're contributing to the lives of our kids when in fact, we are not. We can get very accustomed to this sort of self-deception. The only antidote is radical self-honesty.

How do you know if you are a well-meaning, but "do nothing" parent? *If you have the greatest intentions in the world, but your son is still not going anywhere.* Your intentions are only as good as the outcome they generate. The literal meaning of your intentions are in the response they generate from others. If your son is not visibly improving, or moving in a positive direction, then you are doing something wrong. Be radically honest with yourself.

Screw-up #2: No Vision/No Plan

There is a story about of a group of dignitaries who were visiting the newly opened Disney World in Orlando, Florida, sometime after the death of Walt Disney. Walt Disney's son was conducting the tour, during which a member of the entourage commented how sad it was that Walt had died without seeing the finished attraction. Walt Disney's son stopped a moment to think, then replied, "He did see it when it was completed; that's why it's here."

Too many of us live completely by accident. "Life by default," I call it. That's when life just happens to you; No plan, no system, no vision. Letting the forces of Life—force your life. People who are stuck in this trap are what we all are afraid to be. We tend to be voyeurs on our visions of tomorrow. It's popular these days to visualize things that we want, but we end up watching those visualizations on television. We wait for others to act for us, never understanding the importance of getting into the action of making our own vision and plans happen.

The troubling part is, if you don't decide what your visions and plans are someone *will* decide for you! Do you really want this to happen? In your job and obligations, someone has a plan for spending your time and your resources if you don't. Someone or something is always willing to tell you what to do.

Being told what to do is all right in proper circumstances. But parents should be especially wary. Your best intentions are not necessarily what the world values, and your son is *not* on the white world's list of top priorities. The white people holding power in this world have their own agendas and priorities, and are making sure *their* obligations get done! Your son isn't on their list.

Screw-up #3: "Bolts-in-the-Neck" Parenthood

We are all familiar with the classic tale of Frankenstein. He is that pieced together guy with a hot-temper and a bad tailor! He was more or less the creation of a brilliant scientist who thought that you could create life by an odd combination of surgery and lightning. Does this relate to parenting? Many of our parenting plans are just as pieced together as poor old Frankenstein! We take a little time here, a little effort there, and we sew it together and call it "parenthood." Get the picture? The only thing missing is the bolts in the neck!

If your parenting fits together like Frankenstein, don't be surprised if your kids run away screaming! The approach many parents take to raising their kids would in any other generation be considered neglect. We never seem to commit our "first fruits," our very best time and effort to the task. Instead, we blame other factors like jobs and schedules, the white man, and continue on in our merry way!

The qualities of a good worker and a good parent can seem contradictory.

Qualities Needed for a Successful Career:	*Qualities Needed To Be A Successful Parent:*
1. Long hours and ones best energy.	1. Time to be together as a family for the hard task of parenting.
2. Mobility.	2. Stability.
3. A prime commitment to oneself.	3. Selflessness; Commitment to others.
4. Efficiency.	4. A tolerance for chaos.
5. A controlling attitude.	5. An ability to let go.
6. A drive for high performance.	6. An acceptance of difference and failure.
7. Orientation toward the future.	7. An appreciation of the moment.
8. A goal-oriented, time pressured approach to the task at hand.	8. An ability to tie the same pair of shoelaces twenty-nine times with patience and humor.

It's easy to predict what will happen if you're constantly pressing these two sets of demands together. Your parenting will be pieced together, partially rotted, and very ugly.

Screw-up #4: The Lights Are On And No One's Home

"Pop" psychology in America today is a large, profitable industry and it must continue creating new product lines to stay in business. Part of the "sell" of their products is to convince the public that what they're doing is wrong, and that the new way is a better way.

The "New Way" typically adds little except baseless philosophy, silly therapies, and unsatisfying lifestyles. How so many people can believe this stuff without bursting into laughter is beyond me! It is because we too easily relinquish our own ability to think and go peacefully with the flow of the popular.

Thoughtlessness among parents usually takes the form of fuzzy-mindedness. We often lack clear, thoughtful rationale for the actions we undertake. It can be as simple as neglecting to think about the impact of our beliefs and actions, to a willful abandonment of critical thought. We often simply choose to judge the correctness of new parenting ideas according to the latest prevailing fad. This herd mentality is responsible for a substantial amount of family chaos.

Screw-up #5: Letting Time Steal Your Life

The mismanagement of time steals away your life in sneaky ways. Time is an experienced flyer: The kids grow up too fast, there's never enough moments to do what you want to do, and before you stop to notice, life has glided quietly out the back door.

First it robs by orienting our obsession with the "here and now," to the detriment of the future. The present moment, has a compelling almost gravitational rein on our attention. We never seem to escape it long enough to plan for tomorrow, let alone to leave a legacy for the generations to follow. The energy to plan for the future seems to bleed through the cuts of the moment. Time taunts us. Precious, irreplaceable time is squandered by just getting through our day. What's worse is that not only is our time stolen, but sometimes we aren't even aware that it's gone. . .!

What does time do to our beliefs? What will you believe to be true ten years from now? Will it be what you believe today? Try thinking about what was important ten years ago. Have *those* beliefs changed? Most likely the answer is yes. With imperceptible slowness life seems to creep and change. We shed layer after layer of our beliefs like a snake shedding his skin and all without even a blink of awareness. This is the chief operating mode of the thief of time.

Here is another angle: The next ten, twenty, thirty years will bring changes we cannot even begin to predict. Our values, beliefs and biases will all undergo sharp changes due to unforeseeable life experiences. This implies that the goals you set today will be made without even the slightest ability to predict what you might drift into tomorrow! This fact will create problems of compromised commitments, quivering aims, and drifting goals. Not because we are bad people, mind you, but because time is sweeping past and we haven't the means to harness it. This problem requires a swift response. The time to start is now. Your African American young man won't be young long.

▦ **CHAPTER 5**
The Unconventional Path

*Every race and every nation should be judged by
the best it has been able to produce, not by the
worst.*

—James Weldon Johnson

There once was a story about a group of people that were going on a wilderness exploration in Africa. They arrived at the camp on the edge of the jungle, and spent the morning preparing packs and supplies for the long trek. But, there was problem. A member of the expedition noticed that the guide did not have the map for the area they were going to explore! No maps! And to make matters worse, no compass! With growing worry, they anxiously approached the guide but he just looked confidently at them and smiled. "Maps and compasses are not the way through the jungle," he announced. "*I* am the way."

The unconventional pathway to raising African American men, into good Black men, is you! You're tailored to the task. Raised to it and bred with the ideals for it, since childhood, even though you don't know it yet. What you do know is that you can *recognize distinction when you see it.* You recognize excellence, when it's in front of you. You can spot the above average quickly. *That,* my friend, is the beginning of raising African American man.

I would like to offer five unconventional replies to the screw-ups of parenthood. They will help keep you on the unconventional path:

1. Keep the unconventional path simple
2. You can stretch further than you think
3. African American young men need coaches, mentors, and heroes
4. Your attitude is the defining factor
5. It 'don't' pay to quit

Keep the Unconventional Path Simple

In clinical medicine, the most difficult job is *diagnosing* an illness. That's the part that requires the most talent and intuition. The treatments are routine, and somewhat easy to apply. They're even listed in a book for easy reference!

Raising winners is just the opposite. "Diagnosing" what children might need to grow is fairly easy, and deciding on a course of action is simple. It's the "treatment" that takes talent and intuition. Such is the case with raising winners.

There are an astronomical number of choices to make when interacting with your son. Some of the choices are simple and some aren't. Don't take the complexity of this lightly because, choices often determine the success of your relationship.

It's disturbingly complex with an incalculable numbers of options and choices. Should you play it safe, or do something radical? Risk going all out, or become as conservative as possible to avoid error and trouble? These, and other questions, must be answered. What is the correct option to choose? That is sometimes unanswerable. This much we can be sure of however; the more choices you avail yourself to the better are your chances of selecting a successful course. Fear of change is the most prominent cause of lack of options from which to choose.

You can Stretch Further than You Think

You can stretch the performance of any of your senses or abilities, just like you physically stretch your body. You can stretch your imagination, your drive, your stubbornness, your love, and your patience. Stretching yourself is a core element in delivering your best effort to your son. Your best is often measured by how far you can stretch.

You can always do more than you think you can. Can you do everything? Of course not. We're real world people and we know that personal stretching does have its limits. All you can do, is all you can do. But, you can push yourself sensibly and stretching yourself in areas that have a high probability of impact. Stretch yourself wisely and do a few things exceptionally well.

African American Young Men Need Coaches, Mentors and Heroes

When children are born, they need nurturing, a form of motherly care that fathers cannot offer. Dad's role is limited physically at the start, except to play a support role for mother and what she is doing. However Dad's importance grows after the first few years of life.

As your son grows through the first five years of life, the scene begins to change. African American young men begin to have a need for what a dad can offer in a role that mothers can't fulfill. African American young men don't need mothering daddy's. They have need for a Black man that is decisive, fun, and willing to stand up and be counted. They need coaches, mentors, and heroes.

A coach is someone who teaches, inspires, cajoles, demands, encourages, pushes and leads. Good coaches can create great performances in ordinary people. We build statues to, and heap great honor on those who have the patience and strength to mold men and women into champions. It's a great virtue to create (coach) people in sports or life, who "play over their heads," "reach for the stars," and are willing to work for their dreams.

African American young men also need mentors. A mentor is a tutor and a model; somebody with a special interest in the young man, a skill to teach, and a willingness to do so. Interestingly, most African American young men will seek out adult Black men to fulfill this relationship in their lives. It can be you, if you choose to be available.

Most caretakers sense that it is normal for African American young men to be mentored, but don't know how to naturally fulfill the need. They have no specific knowledge about how to model things for their little apprentices, or how to set standards, or even how to make *themselves* into someone specific and special. *It is* urgent to help the mom's and dad's who are floundering in this pool of confusion.

What about heroes? Do you remember those old war movies where there are a group of soldiers, squatting in a foxhole, and in comes a live grenade? All eyes bulge in fear, as a mad scramble erupts. Just before detonation, one brave soul thoughtlessly and selflessly dives on the thing, losing his life and making himself an instant legend. Events like this have actually happened, and the stories of real heroic exploits are riveting. Why? Who are these people that jump on grenades? They're heroes. They don't have grand ideologies or complex motives. We immortalize their demonstration of courage and immortal action, but they don't see themselves as special. They see a job, and do it. Their anesthetic for the pain they often endure is *caring*. They're perfectly willing to sacrifice themselves for those they care about.

We need heroes like that now! You're probably the only *hero* your African American young man will ever personally know. You love your son intensely and would be willing to sacrifice your life for his. After all his life is more important than your own.

My personal foundation dictates that I place my kids importance above my own. I cannot escape this bias, and I know it communicated through the things I say. You have the obligation to examine this value carefully, before we begin and decide for yourself, if this is one philosophy that you care to embrace.

Please make a conscious decision to accept this value. Until you do, the final level of commitment to your son will pitch and waver. There's no room for that: the final outcome of your effort will be placed in certain jeopardy.

God has designed us all to need something worth living for. It is the motivational root for heroism. Your kids didn't choose you, and you didn't choose them but by some divine providence, you're together for life, and nothing you can do or say will change that. They need someone to be their hero, because the world will be cruel to them. Make your move.

Your Attitude Is *The* Defining Factor

This idea might not sound stirring or unconventional on the surface, but consider this exemplary and wise story:

> *An old black farmer was out working in the fields when along down the road came a tired looking Black man.*
> *"Where ya' goin' stranger?" The farmer asked.*
> *The man leaped back, startled, and with a trembling voice and bulging eyes replied,*
> *"T-T-To de next town . . . What those people like in de next town?" "What were da like in de last town?" the farmer asked.*
> *"Da was all mean and cruel, I didn't like dem at all"*
> *The stranger blurted.*
> *The farmer sadly shook his head and looked down.*
> *"You'll find de people of the next town to be the same way."*
> *A few days later, another Black man came down the same road.*
> *"How ya' doin' stranger?" The farmer asked, to which the stranger replied,*
> *"Very good if da Lord willin' sir."*
> *"Say, what do you know of da people in the next town?" The stranger asked. The farmer looked at him for a moment and asked wisely,*
> *"What were da like in the last town you were in?"*
> *"OH MY!! They were very friendly and kind to me, and I enjoyed dem very much!" Replied the stranger. A smile came to the farmers face and he said,*
> *"You'll find da people of the next town to be just exactly the same way . . ."*

What type of attitude does your son have?

It Don't Pay to Quit . . .

Don't ever forget that the world *wants* you to quit.

I have days where I feel terribly lazy. I get mad, I get distracted and irritable, I get in ruts and I'm proved wrong. Confusion and intimidation are my frequent colleagues but, I don't quit.

I never quit; I can't. Neither should you, even in your lowest moments. If you have one motto from which you never sway, it should be "It don't pay to quit." Such should be the credo of all parents.

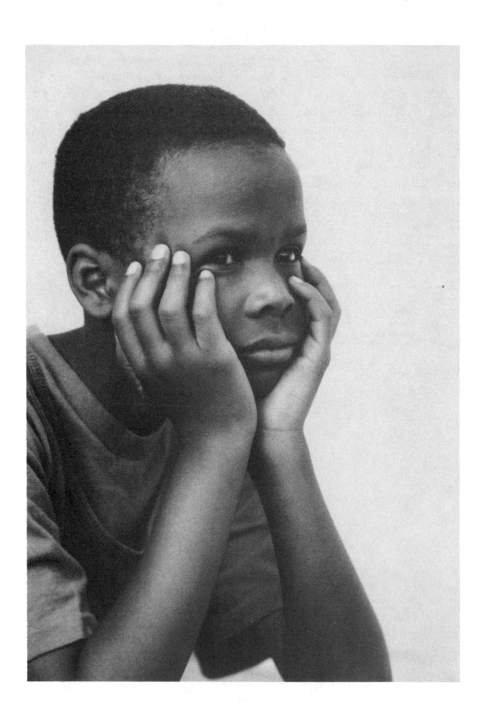

▓ CHAPTER 6

What Stops African American Young Men from Succeeding?

It grew on me that we, Black men especially, we expected to be subservient even in groups where ostensibly everyone was equal.

—Shirley Chisholm

The worst way to fail on the African American journey is to be stopped. If you want to win, find out how your problems operate, and set about preparing for them. If you know what's coming and prepare, you and your son cannot be stopped.

Healthy manhood is a normal thing to grow toward, so asking how to get there is a strange question. A more sensible perspective would be to analyze the detours that could tempt him on his journey to Black manhood. This is such a refreshing perspective! What will stop your son from naturally gaining his full potential as a Black man? What styles or habits should be avoided to stay on the natural road to black manhood? What about you, the cheerleader along the road? How might you unintentionally hinder his success?

These are wonderful questions that only make sense within a common understanding about what constitutes victory. I want my sons to win, and I'm sure you do too. Let's look at what will stop your son from developing to his maximum in manhood, and what you can do to make sure your son has the best opportunities to develop successfully.

How Shall We Think of Success?

I've had my appreciation of this effort magnified by working with professional athletes. I can tell you as a first hand witness that what hard working, committed athletes display on Sunday television, is the result of effort and pressure that the average person cannot fathom. Most of us just don't specifically know how to think and act like a winner. Even though we all must fight daily for a job, or promotions, we never stop to consider what it takes to achieve real victory. Understanding victory begins with a conversation about competition.

Our world is organized by the outcome of countless competitions. There are generally two different forms of competitions. First, there are competitions against ourselves; and second there are competitions against others. Competition against ourself are a challenge like getting out of bed in the morning and maintaining our ideal weight.

Competition against other people, are a different class of competition. These competitions are activities like: getting a good parking spot, persuading people to see things your way, or fighting for some time alone. If you stop and think about it you invest your time everyday in some form of competitive exercise. Most of these competitions are normal and serve the general purpose of living in life.

Now enter "winning." The white world is like a ruthless fight promoter. It doesn't care if you win or lose, it just wants to see a good fight! The world is responsible for defining "winning" and is defined as how well you *compare* to someone else. Winning means having competition that conclude in your favor. For better or worse, we learn to focus on our relative position to others.

The unfortunate problem is that true victory and success ultimately need to be based on assessments you make about yourself, internally and emotionally, without anyone else's perspective. In the final analysis, the judgement of how successful you have been, rests on whether or not you have lived up to what you believe to be your own capabilities.

Some of us have been winning our whole life. Yet, we look in the mirror and know we could do better. Others, have been losers their whole life, but know deep down that they gave it all they had! Who do you think **feels** more successful?

The ultimate evaluation about whether your life is successful will come when you compare your life, against your talent and potential. It won't come by highlighting your successes; it won't come by counting the number of cars in your garage or measuring the gold chains; and it won't come by focusing solely on your mistakes and faults. Ultimately, it will be just you and the person in the mirror, and at that instant you are going to make a judgement about what you could have been, despite the obstacles.

Your choice will be simple. Did you give life your best effort? To say "yes" will produce a sense of gratification that is reserved for your wildest dreams. To say "no" condemns you to a life of bitterness and second guessing. Perhaps you are familiar with a piece of research that was done on retirees in a nursing home with respect to what they regretted most in life. By a large margin the most commonly reported regret was "not taking enough chances in life." *Translation: "I wish I should have, would have, could have."*

"Did I give it my best?" is a deep personal evaluation. Nobody can answer this for you. Only you know what your dreams are, and what potential you are capable of, so only you can answer that question.

Your sons want to be successful like people they know. Inside each of their hearts kindle dreams, and desires, you or I know nothing about.

African American young men naturally model themselves after who they see doing, what they aspire to.

Unless taught otherwise, they will judge their success based upon the white fantasy world's external standards of relative position. This myth will never give them the sense of achievement and success they naturally strive for. Only a deep appreciation of their own talents and a consistent effort to stretch themselves will provide any long term satisfaction.

A Special Note to Parents

Life has dealt you one hand of cards, a son, and you must play him as smartly as you can. No second chances so listen carefully:

Teaching your son to compete against himself is really very simple. You start by determining; A) what does he think he's capable of; B) how far he has come along *that* road; and C) what is going to stop him from getting where he wants to go? Answer those questions and you will have helped him create a very effective method of applying his energy.

We all have ideas of what we want to do in our lives, and chances are good that your son has some wild plans. At this point in his life, the wilder the better. Encourage him to think big. Don't tell him what to think, just make whatever it is BIG! Avoid squishing the ridiculous sounding things that he might dream up. The world has plenty of cold water to throw on his fire without you adding your own. Besides, he might surprise you. At this point your job is to coach him through the first stage of "getting out of life what he wants." Teach him to dream very big and bold!

What's going to stop him from getting those dreams? Plenty.

You and Your Son Are on a Tuff Road

What will *stop* your son from getting where he wants to go? If you effectively anticipate this answer, **You cannot be stopped**! You can prepare and plan around all the defeating influences.

If you think you can effectively negotiate this tricky road alone, I salute your courage. But, I don't want you to fail.

Let's assume that there is an "upper limit" to what you as a parent can do for your son. That means there is a point where you have done all that you can humanly do, to help your son. You can do no more after this point except cut him loose and pray to the Lord. When does that "cut-loose" time arrive? Soon, all too soon.

If there is an upper limit to what you can do, then it's logical that *there is only so much that you can do*. You only have your son for a few years of his life, and the impact you can have is limited physically. You must try to reach the upper limit of what you can do as quickly as possible. The clock is running! Many factors are now at work to keep you from reaching that theoretical "upper limit."

Knowing specifically, what will stop each of your movements provides a "location map" of the land mines that can blow you both off the road. Having this map can be the source of great confidence and boldness! It focuses your attention. It also provides a sensible way for you to apply your energy to skirting around potential disasters and to confidently proceed on the road to victory.

The forces that will stop your son are:

A. Lack of a plan
B. Ignoring whether he's getting what he wants
C. Being inflexible in his personal behavior

D. Having small dreams
E. Bad Company

A. Lack of a Plan

I have already spoken to some extent about how this pitfall effects parenting. As for your son, the most troubling aspect involves two problems: First, without a clear plan he has no idea what he's trying to accomplish, and therefore has no way of measuring whether he's successful. African American young men need to be told it's time to accomplish specific goals. They don't think much about tomorrow. They must be trained to learn how, to set up a goal, and how to reach it and evaluate their progress. A simple, written plan serves this simple objective.

Second, if he doesn't have a direction or plan, he can't respond to the roadblocks and troubles. *If your African American young man doesn't know what he's trying to accomplish with his efforts, the troubles in his life will make no sense.* Normal everyday challenges will make him feel picked on, or victimized by white society if he has no plan. Normal everyday challenges will suddenly make lots of sense when he sees that they are stopping him from getting something specific in his life! He can see the problems as thwarting his progress, toward a specific end. That kind of problem is much easier to respond to than one that comes out of a race hating society for no apparent reason.

By the way, I *don't* see any purpose in making your son into a goal driven type "A" monster. That's not what childhood is about. But, being totally without any organized thought about tomorrow is equally unfair. This may sound somewhat contradictory, but you handicap your son by allowing him to remain a child indefinitely, and you handicap him by forcing his growth. It's a delicate balance that wise parents must strike.

A *mission sentence* allows you to dance on the fine line between the two extremes. A mission sentence summarizes what your son wants to do with his tomorrows. It gives him focus and grounds him. It should be clear enough to suggest a course of action, and provide a means of measurement for verifying his achievement.

The secret is to make your son create an absurdly simple sentence and post it someplace. "I want to have fun today," written in dry-erase marker on the bathroom mirror will do nicely (It comes off with easily). The point is not so much to create a grand plan for life (he's a child, remember?) but to introduce your son to the *idea* of a plan. It should be specific enough to provide an idea about what he might want to achieve, but broad enough to allow for change. Try things like "I want to beat someone in a race," or "I want to save $10 for my new sneaks" and so on. Keep it simple. Let your son create his own sentences. Let him have as many as he likes. These mission sentences simply create standards to reach for. It reminds your son what he wants, and what he needs to get there. Don't haggle over wording; let him do it his way. Better to have a misworded goal than to have none at all.

Ask your son about the headway he's making on his missions. Make it a point to remind him of what he stated he wanted to do, and ask if there is anything you can do to help. Asking him to measure his progress on the personal mission sentence is imperative. How else can your son know if he needs to be working differently to reach his goal? Reviewing goals is a task that is snubbed in everyday life. We need to teach our sons to analyze frequently "how" they are doing.

B. Ignoring the Analysis of Outcomes

Have you ever stopped to think about whether or not what you are doing is working? Strange as it may seem, it's rare for people to stop and say to themselves "is what I am doing getting me where I want to go?" Why else would so many of us continue doing things that clearly are not getting us anywhere?

This is a notorious trap of African American young men. It's stops excellence with a thud.

I want to suggest a rule that you teach to your son immediately: **If what you are doing is not working, do**

something different!!! This idea might sound idiotically simple. It is. Perhaps that's the reason so many miss it. If your son thinks some procedure or idea is supposed to work a certain way, he will blindly believe it without checking, whether or not it actually works in practice.

This is particularly true in attaining goals or solving problems. Teach your son to understand that even priceless advice you think is fail safe, will fail from time to time! I guarantee that everything that works like a charm for me, or you, will not always have the same effect for your son. He needs to have the patience to try different avenues if what is supposed to work, fails. Constantly prod him with the question: "Is that what you wanted. . . ?" He must analyze the "outcome" of his behavior to answer your question. If he finds that what is supposed to work is failing, inform him that he has permission to be as creative, and as relentless as necessary to succeed.

C. Being Inflexible in His Personal Behavior

Along similar lines like not noticing outcomes, is to stubbornly retain inflexibility in behavior. People-changers will tell you that the major hurdle in helping others grow is developing new behaviors; new ways of thinking and acting. People get "cliched" in their behavior and won't try anything new. Sons in particular gravitate into "grooves" or patterns of behaving, and don't try new things. This leads to stagnation and atrophy in their lives. African American young men can then become robots, who are unable to dream up or perform any fresh sort of action. This will make them sad and unhappy, even though they may be unable to express it.

D. Having Small Dreams

Dreaming for the future is something that normally evaporates with advancing manhood. That happens when dreams get stomped on, without an adult to prop up or to encourage you. At the core of this trouncing is the reality that it's easier to dream things up than to actually have them. Sure, most eight year olds want to play in the NBA, but the reality of getting there, is different than the dreaming. We've all gone through it, and for that reason we all feel the pain our sons experience, when they get their cherished hopes and dreams dashed away.

To protect them from this excessive pain, we encourage them to so something damaging. Dream "realistically" we call it. If you do this with your son, you carelessly stomp out one of God's greatest fires. In a thousand "realistic ways" we crush imagination and big dreams, and make our sons read off of our own agenda in life. While they are still young and pliable, light their fuse and get out of the way!!

Let their minds soar and fly to places beyond your imagination. Encourage them to *forget being realistic.* After all, where has your "realistic" imagination taken you? Perhaps we would all do well to emulate these child dreamers, rather than choke them with pre-mature maturity. Encourage them to dream BIG! But plan well.

E. Bad Company

I don't think much has to be said about this. Bad company corrupts good character. Birds of a feather flock together— water seeks its own level.

My son was hanging around with some bad characters so I told him a story. I told him the story about the guy who was hiking up the mountain, when this cobra came out of the weeds. The cobra asked if he could have a ride to the top of the mountain, because his stomach was sore. The man was smart and said, "No, you're a snake and you'll bite me." The snake calmly assured the hiker that he would not bite him if he would just give him a ride. The hiker finally agreed, and up they went.

When they got to the top of the mountain, the hiker went to put the cobra down, and the snake reared back and bit him on the hand! The hiker leaped back with shock and fell to the ground. Dying of the venom. With bulging disbelief in his eyes and fear in his voice, he screamed, "Why did you bite me! You promised you wouldn't bite me and now I'm going to die!!" The snake curled his evil lips and hissed, "you knew I was a snake when you picked me up. Snakes lie and snakes bite . . ." My kids are free to choose their friends. They are not free, (as you can imagine) to be free of my opinion and input. They are under strict agreement with me "not to come crying when the snake they are carrying around, bites."

Your son may not readily accept your opinion of his pals, so don't expect it. Thank goodness, sons don't want trouble, they just want fun and friends. Bad company usually show their stripes quickly, making it possible to teach about friendship at clear and opportune moments. If a particular friend is being a jerk, remind him of the cobra. It's fairly easy to encourage your son, on to better people. There are plenty of good people around if he determines to find them.

If You Could only Teach Him One Thing. . .

If you could teach your son only one thing in his life, teach him self-discipline. Lets' define it as making yourself do things you would rather not do. Self discipline, is like an artery running through every aspect of his life, feeding and nourishing what it can reach. Like a developing circulatory system, an unseen source of life in a new baby, make self discipline a part of all that he does.

Let's extend this metaphor. Lack of self-discipline is a common feature of all African American young men. The extent of this lack of discipline is what might surprise you. If left completely on his own, your son won't do much more than make himself comfortable. Just like in an artery, growth is something that you must circulate into every area of his life including: work, studying, friendships, honesty, commitment, chivalry and several others. The force must be you.

I'll be talking about these areas as this book unfurls. For now understand that to miss the chance to learn self-discipline today, guarantees massive difficulty in the future. I know because I've suffered from it. Perhaps you have too. This book rests on a fulcrum of evolving self discipline, and the many ways "it" leads your son into a successful future. Think on this as you read the following pages.

▦ CHAPTER 7
What is Stopping Parents from Succeeding?

Keep hope alive.

—Rev. Jesse Jackson

No one can save us, from us, but us.

—Rev. Jesse Jackson

I'll Get to the Point! *Raising Winners is like running for a touchdown in a football game. It's acceptable to get tackled when you can see what's happening, but it's aggravating to get blindsided one-yard from the goal line. You don't want to look back on this part of your life and say "if only I had known." This will help you see, what you may not know as it is about to tackle you.*

Trickle Down Parents

It should be of no great revelation, that what effects you, good or bad has a trickle down effect on your children. Separating your lives from theirs is impossible. For that reason I've included this short discussion to highlight those factors that will stop you from reaching the "upper limits" of influence on your children.

You're Just Ignorant—So Get Critical

Honest ignorance of helpful knowledge, is the major obstacle for you to "doing all you can do." We all possess reasonable intelligence, agreed? If there is an architecture for "failure" in raising winners, it's a lack of culture or stolen heritage, that makes us ignorant of useful information in making intelligent and powerful choices. Having a view, or knowledge of, our complete historical heritage will provide the foundation for reaching the upper limits of powerful positive Black influence!

I have personal and troubling fears in certain areas of my life about the lack of knowledge concerning my African heritage. It also worries me that my knowledge of our culture might be too shallow, to save the life of one of my kids today's white dominated society. It worries me that my grasp of our changing social status, and our growing business trends might be too weak to seize the opportunities available. It worries me that our cultural passion for basketball might harm our future. If I'm ignorant of cultural information, I might be missing something I need to change the course of the lives of my many African American brothers and sisters.

Reading this book suggests you have an above average level of concern about what is happening to our black males. I trust my instincts and observations, and I would encourage you to trust your instincts as well. Most of us are the product of a white American segregated school system. We learned to be passive recipients of racial domination. Too little of our formal education was focused on questioning, challenging, and learning innovative aspects to be our best. Public school education, for many African Americans, often punished us for thinking on our own and trusting what made sense. It rather rewarded us for staying in "straight lines" and being "cooperative," behaving like good "Negroes."

Disagreements by Black male students are often interpreted, as an open challenge to white authorities! This can lead to embarrassment and insult, the two nightmares of Black childhood. To deal with that, Black males just shut their heads off, do what they are told, and give the cool sign of indifference.

Be careful if this was your training; you've learned something you must fight to overcome. You're no dunce if you can't stand on your two feet and develop a reasoned opinion. You've just never had the opportunity. Lucky for you, your brain developed through application, even when the opportunity was denied by white society.

We must learn to apply our brain and trust its products. The best way to apply our brain is to become a critical thinker. Somehow, your brain erupts in activity when you challenge mentally the things you are told. This is easy to do, but requires a wee-bit of effort.

The following information is most useful and powerful if read critically. This means, that you think through these ideas, evaluate the logic, challenge the thinking if necessary, think of examples of applications in your home, and consider the implications. Better for you to reject something on this list because you thought it was senseless, than to do it, because I said so.

Now, do everything I say and don't ask questions! This section suggests what will impede you from successfully coaching your Black male through the up-hill journey. Memorizing this list won't deposit the information in the part of your brain that needs it. Critical thinking will.

The forces that will stop *you* are:

A. Being unaware of natural biological development
B. Your attitudes toward your son
C. Imposing your will and desire
D. Lack of personal/parental discipline

Being Unaware of Natural Biological Developments

Guiding and impact for our black males requires a sensitivity about what changes in your son naturally develop over time and how these changes progress. These biologically driven developments go on in full view, but you may have little recognition of them and less control.

You need a quick overview of child development. Not a college version, but an "in-the-trenches," boot camp version. Understanding simple biological changes that are happening within our black males can provide knowledge in, what you can and cannot control. You can then cleanly hurdle another block on the road to building great black males. When an age specific observation is in order, I'll mention it. If some aspect of thinking or behaving shifts or changes with age, I shall mention that as well.

One quick observation is in order. After observing thousands of black children and parents, I've concluded that "Chips off the ole' block" are rare. Unless a mother sees a fault in her son and says, "You're no good just like your dad." You could be the most sedate and controlled individual in the world and have a totally wild animal for a son. "He's like his dad, the old M.F.!" you would assure yourself! On the other hand are kids who are quiet and frail born to loud, burly and quarrelsome parents. Where did *this* kid come from? The bad seed. Who knows? Don't be too concerned if your son is a lot like you or very different from you. If there is a similarity, it's only an illusion! You are who you are, and he is who he is.

All the general developments I am going to discuss will go on in spite of you. I have discovered that what frightens parents most are the normal and natural consequences of development they don't know about. These changes are to a large extent, biologically governed and subject to little outward manipulation. I really think this is God's way of insuring that we can't mess up our kids! Thankfully, you can't really alter any of these biological parameters even if you tried.

The Development of African American Young Men's Thinking

Nobody wants to think that their son is deficient, yet a great deal of parental anxiety swirls around this fear. Particularly, when their son acts, for lack of a better term, like a "butthead." You probably know the feeling of sadly shaking your head at your son and thinking, "Oh no, my kid is a fool!" Parents really need a simple understanding of the development of logic and general intelligence.

But be forewarned. I am going to be rifling through a topic that occupies volumes of scientific theory and fact. What you are getting is the boiled down treatment necessary to operate effectively. If you want further reading on this topic, you will find suggested readings at the back of the book.

Natural biological development constrains Black men to progress from infantile thinking to adult-style thinking, over the five to twelve year range. They start this phase of life thinking in very concrete, "here-and-now" sensory based acquisition of knowledge. This is very different from how you and I think. As maturity proceeds, in fits and starts, black males improve their ability to think abstractly (thinking in the absence of sensory input) finally, going over a "hump" between eight and eleven years old. Higher forms of adult-style logic, then become possible. Just remember that mature minds are a result of biological growth in a slow, stuttered fashion.

Behaviors related to this stuttered development and the "hump" really drive parents crazy. Around the 3rd and 4th grade, Black men go through a trying transition. "Good sense" and "good judgement" are qualities we expect in an adult frame of thinking. At times don't expect these from your son for he is unable to consistently or effectively think in these ways.

Black men can only solve problems that they can get their hands on. They have a hard time with conceptual matters like common sense, abstract reasoning, and thinking ahead until the tail end of the teen phase of life. These qualities are way beyond what young men right now can "grasp."

General intelligence is a different story. It too has a developmental pattern, and also relates to the development of abstract reasoning ability. But I need to introduce an important twist. Many parents get concerned about their son's Intelligence Quotient (IQ), and there are many misunderstandings that deserves clarification.

The IQ is a measurement representing, a ratio of chronologically based age and measures of mental ability. In the collective white public mind, IQ indicates how white your kid is, not how smart. It's the method they have for comparing one another. In the last few years, there has developed a controversy about what the scores really indicate. Critics feel (and there are many critics!) that the accepted tests of IQ measure only certain kinds of social intelligence. The critics challenge the general validity of the tests claiming that they only test verbal/mathematical intelligence. The more skilled a child is with white written language and logic, the better (s)he will perform on the test. Therefore, they say IQ is not a fair or accurate measurement for Black males whose use of formal language may differ, but the look of intelligence is the same.

The implication here is that there are many measurements of intelligence. IQ scores are just one. It is unfair that Black males who are extremely intelligent do not test as well on the most practical form used to measure general intelligence, the IQ score. Leading to a conclusion that IQ scores are generally biased.

Howard Gardner, a well respected and prolific Harvard psychologist, presents some radical ideas in his book *Frames of Mind*. He suggests an appealing alternative to this crude method of classifying intelligence. In this book, he suggests that there are at least six different types of intelligence which can be used to measure people! Everybody has all of these measures to some greater or lesser extent. That means that everybody is good at some of them, and not so good at others.

The six intelligences are these:

A. Linguistic Intelligence
B. Musical Intelligence
C. Logical-Mathematical Intelligence
D. Spatial Intelligence
E. Bodily-Kinesthetic Intelligence
F. The Personal Intelligences

Let's consider each of these.

The linguistic intelligence includes your ability to use and understand the native language. This includes speaking, understanding nuances, innuendo, synonyms, and your ability to be creative with words. Perhaps you know of people who are gifted in this intelligence, like speakers, writers, storytellers, and rappers.

Musical intelligence represents a special form of intelligence with respect to sound. Musical intelligence can be expressed as having good pitch perception, a sense of rhythm, tempo, and accurate recognition along with production of timbre (specific qualities of a tone.)

Logical-Mathematical intelligence is having skill with numbers, manipulating sets of figures and pieces by a pattern of rules, and applying symbolic reasoning. Einstein was considered a rather dull student because he didn't begin to speak till very late in his life. But his logical-mathematical brilliance allowed him to make several great contributions in his field.

Spatial intelligence reflects a great command of dimensional space. Those with spatial intelligence have a good sense of depth, can imagine things in many (more than three) dimensions, and generally have a great degree of sensitivity about what is around them. This may not sound like an "intelligence" alone, but consider the difficulty you might have with ordinary life without the ability to think and problem solve in 3-dimensions, or perceive and understand the relationship between objects in your environment.

Bodily-kinesthetic intelligence is sport aptitude and physical ability. This sort of intelligence represents an ability to move their body through space, and to sense and feel the interactions between body and environment. Athletes are therefore brilliant. Michael Jordan is a genius. This should reorient our thinking about "dumb black jocks" because our people are expressing superiority in an unusual area of intelligence. The personal intelligence could easily be rephrased as the "interpersonal intelligence." These are the people that are good with other people. They can sense moods, attitudes, intentions and motivations of others. This intelligence has a high degree of observability and varies widely among black males.

I think you can see that given this list, we might be guilty of being a little snobbish about "intelligence." It wanders over a wide range of qualities, and to say that white is better than black is foolish. Each black male has at least one area in which he excels. He has at least one in which he lacks talent. Be fair with him. Be fair with our race.

A Black Male's Acting

Is there anything normal about the way a black males acts? Thankfully, yes! We can look at the acting in two ways; one is personal behavior, and the other is social behavior.

Curiosity highlights *personal behavior*. This unbridled mental energy makes black males tinker and explore all things. They talk to themselves, try to discover what strange things they can do with their bodies, misuse toys, and a host of other exploration type activities. They are also destructive, because of a lack of self importance. They try to destroy things around them. Just keep in mind that your son is on a constant search for new worlds to understand, and his wiring causes perpetual, easily annoying activity!

Black males must constantly manage a balancing act between strange new things happening within their small bodies, and strange things happening outside between themselves and white society. All Black males react to this dynamic and confusing situation differently. Their personal intelligences get involved, their fitful and inaccurate ability to think with logic and abstraction get involved, physical metabolism throws in its' wrenches, and of course there is the strong Black mom and dad to deal with! Any wonder the kids act crazy?

For the most part, *social development* during this phase involves learning social skills like, team-work, honesty, self-control, building friendships, and "finding your voice" in the crowd. These developments are rocky roads that bump and bang our Black males to exhaustion. It's worsened by the fact that they don't understand much of what's going on, and need to learn by trial and error. These trials and errors are difficult to grow through, and some never do, so be prepared to be patient.

Prepare yourself for an up hill climb. Your sons friendships form and dissolve sometimes, within hours. Contention and strife, punctuated with periods of peaceful coexistence with parents and friends are normal throughout the whole young Black males' range. "Telling the truth" is a puzzling and tantalizing amusement. Emotional outburst spontaneously occur, leading to embarrassment and shyness. Black males flirt with different patterns of interaction, testing and trying different "looks" to see how they work and feel. Black males need to be somebody's favorite, and go to unusual lengths to secure it. The inferiority complex the white man has given us makes this a must. This period, is a time of great social experimentation, and within reason needs just to be endured. Offer your opinion as frequently as you like, for believe me your son is looking for ideas of things that "work." To help him make friends, fit in, avoid enemies and have fun. And to deal with this complex racial society.

You cannot stop this "social frenzy" as Black males hunt, search and experiment for a style of behavior they can be comfortable with. You can help this naturally driven search by availing yourself to comment on the appropriateness or effect of a certain behavior, or by merely suggesting new alternatives. They are hopelessly dependent upon you for so much, but are continually experimenting with ways to experience freedom and independence.

It is a long and painful up hill road that we all have to travel. The best help you can offer is that of a friend and not strip them of their dignity like the white slave master who belittled and beat our people. I suppose you will agree that fitting in is something we all try to do starting as kids, and we really don't stop until we die. Give them a little help! Show them our great history, so they can see a bright future. Show them that fitting in is not necessary, as long as you are proud of who you are.

Black Males Feelings

"Feelings" are a mystery for psychology. We don't really know what, or why they are, but we do know they make us distinctly human. Some feelings like "anger" and "hatred" and "love" are famous and have books written about them. Other feelings like "pensiveness," "chilling" and "boredom" aren't cool enough to have their own spot on the bookshelf! Understanding feelings among adults is one notch above pure guesswork, so let's be conservative and realistic with ourselves about understanding our sons.

The most dominating (and ominous) pattern parents see in their Black males emotions are the "hiding" of emotions over time. This is very normal and usually means nothing more than your son is gaining self-consciousness, and feels embarrassed to show publicly what he feels. This is all a very normal response to becoming aware of yourself.

I referred earlier to the hump that sons go through around the 3rd to 4th grade. The natural development of self-consciousness is the creator of the hump. Perhaps you remember those initial moments when you knew you were "here." This is a very odd sensation, and most people can recall the strangeness of the experience.

A cloud of ignorance hangs over our understanding of what happens in those moments. We know that as normal brain development proceeds, around the age of 8—10 we gain sudden, flickering perceptions of something "new." We can continue to experience the world as we were before, and we also can step outside, and see ourselves as the world sees us. "Self-consciousness" we call it. It is a profound important event that marks the beginning of adult thinking about self worth.

This change will also effect many areas of behavior. The nature of blackness shifts noticeably when we pass into self-consciousness. The previous pattern of experimentation continues with this newfound awareness of who we really are, creating all sorts of new situations. We can suddenly be introspective and wonder about important matters of concern, we can read white peoples' motives and intentions for the first time, and we see ourselves as others see us, as niggers for the first time.

Emotions become objects in addition to being experiences, and we are suddenly aware of the difference between ourself and the world around us. It's a paradoxical experience for most of us because it's frightful, interesting, confusing, tantalizing and inescapable. Black males usually don't talk much about it, but the effects are evident in how they act.

New personality traits could also crop up. Periods of quietness and reclusiveness are common. A new found attention to appearances can also be expected. The social patterns of your Black male will change. All this might make you a bit uncomfortable.

It's normal for parents to dread any new state of development in our kids. Even if the development is normal. The emotional hiding that African American young men go through expressed as self-consciousness can be terrifying, because we have been programmed by the Black culture to view hiding emotions as "bad." It's not. It is in fact, very normal.

Black males are very tough, so don't get shook up. The passage into self-consciousness is extraordinarily interesting and to date almost totally unexplored. Let it happen. We've all gone through it, and have survived. Don't make your son pay for white society produced insecurities.

Another pattern is exaggeration of feelings. Remember that for the most part, feelings and emotions like: intense hatred, joy, courage, despair, jealously and many others are just being recognized for the first time. Black males tend to play with new things. They do so to varying extremes.

It takes years to learn to modulate powerful feelings, to use them in socially proper ways, and to learn the fine art of self-control. Until that control develops, his emotions will swerve all over the place. Don't faint, just help him. He's not a head case, he's just growing up.

Hidden Implications of Normal Child Development

The first implication is that you are now ready to understand your Black male. If you did nothing more than ingest this information and mix it up with your intelligent day-to-day appraisal of your son, you will be way ahead of most people! *It is your job to be steadfast and unchanging through the swirling waters on his way to manhood.* These young Black men are going to run a game around you and make you talk to yourself incessantly! That's a perfectly normal parental response. They're depending on you to maintain a sensible course in life and model for them temperance, sensibility, and stability, because they have little or none.

Consider yourself the boat, your son will ski behind. He may act crazy and out of control, but he depends on you to stay the course and show him where to go. Your son will go where you pull him.

The second implication is that *it's your role to initiate suggestions for action and his movement to higher levels.* Each crazy phase I listed previously must be traversed, and your leading him on with wisdom and confidence to the next level is pivotal. They will get through it without you, but your help makes the process smoother.

The third implication that arises from these facts is that *psychology is a young science.* The organized, scientific study specifically of African American children is a very young science and there's still much we don't know. The best brightest, and most successful advances in this field are yet to be made! Your observations are as valid as any, and for your child they may be more accurate. Make observations of your African American young male. Study his sleeping patterns, watch what he eats, and look for the connections between disconnected events. Make him the focus of your study. Write down what you see and the changes you sense, and draw your own conclusions. If he starts to experiment with alcohol or drugs, you won't be the last to know.

The fourth implication involves the subtle mechanics of brain performance. *Your African American young man's brain is a solid combination of curious, bright and distractible matter.* Attention spans are very short, and the focus is on the quickly changing landscape of sensory experience. Make your interaction with him short and concrete. Oversimplify your lessons and prepare yourself for feeling like you're not making any difference!

The fifth implication is related to *the amount of your presence, in your son's life.* We don't really know how much or how little you need to be present in order for this "natural" flow to work properly. Quality or quantity time? Moot question. Your son just needs time, all kinds of time. There is no substitute. It's been said that "80% of success is just showing up." Consider this a diamond of wisdom.

Your Attitude Toward Your Son

What you really believe in your heart about your son gets transmitted. *What you believe* can influence power, to form what your son believes. If you think that he is a worthless loser, he'll know it and work toward that level. If you think he is the world's greatest, he will try to live up to that level as well. Black males seem very comfortable and perform better when much is expected.

Get a great big, positive attitude toward your son! Notice how you communicate that feeling. I find that we communicate our attitudes for our sons in two ways: The first is positive. "I want my son to be good with his hands . . ."; "I want my son to be warm and sensitive to women . . ."; and "I want my son to be the President of the United States." Positively stated, positively planned, and positively executed. The second version has a distinctly different sound.

The second version sounds like this: "I just *don't want* my son to be all thumbs . . ."; "I just *don't want* my son to be cold and insensitive to women . . ."; or "I just *don't want* my son to be rejected when he runs for office." Notice the difference? *Telling him what you don't want doesn't tell him what you do want.* It should be obvious that the first version gives a target to shoot at. The second, gives something bad to be avoided. The differences are a world apart.

The most successful people in the world are moving toward a goal with a great attitude (version one) rather than, moving away from a problem (version two.) Too many parents "dream negatively" and can only imagine what they need to *avoid* in life! Observe this in your own attitudes.

Make a decision about what you are going to get in life. The subtlety of your new action will be heard, seen and felt quickly.

How, you ask?

Simple. Version one fills you with confidence, version two fills you with a fear of failure. The first, gives you a clear way of knowing if you've succeeded, the second never allows you the luxury of knowing if you've been successful or not. If you are a dream negative person, your life will seem as though it never gets anyplace. You'll feel stuck, never knowing the achievement you can attain.

Believe in your African American young male no matter how much of a fool he seems to be. Dream big dreams for him, brag about him in front of others, love him and kiss him. Let him know that you have a clear plan for him that will help him get anything in life that he wants. Help him reach for the stars!

CHAPTER 8
Facts of Life

A man's bread and butter is only insured when he works for it.

—Marcus Garvey

Imposing Your Will and Desires

I add this section now for good reason. Similar to establishing a mission sentence for your son, there is a hairline crack between big vision for your son, and imposing your dreams on him, for your own satisfaction. His life is his, and you must accept that, in order to operate in his best interests.

Lack of Personal/Parental Discipline

This could be the greatest *threat to success* in this whole journey. Let me say it simply: It is impossible to ask your son to do something you cannot model for him. If you are unable to discipline yourself, to change some aspect of yourself for your own benefit, then your son will be unable to see the value in improving himself either. *Your level of commitment to being your best will be his.*

Perhaps, you are in the unfortunate situation where all your habits are well structured and in control, but other adults in your sons' life are not. Estranged spouses, grandparents, neighbors and others can all exert a confusing influence. I will offer a simple suggestion that I know is easier to say than to accomplish. You must apply your best effort to align all of the adults in your son's life in the same direction. To the best of your ability, get people to change their bad or contradictory habits.

Enlist and encourage the support of people who unduly influence your son. You will be pleasantly surprised to find you can gain terrific cooperation if you ask, and if it's couched as "for our son." Just ask if they want to help. And keep asking.

Now I Need to Tell You Some Facts of Life . . .

I have spent a much space listing things that pose threats to your success in raising African American young men. This list is of great importance, and should be reviewed often. But I have discovered something very interesting about parents.

I have found that parents feel relief to discover that what they tussle and struggle with are normal, and are exactly what other parents struggle with too! They don't feel so picked on or alone. Because you are not alone! The normal problems, to be expected by us all, are what I consider the "facts of life."

Boiling these down to the "facts of life" is a valuable exercise. These are not intended to hurt or frighten you, but they will in all likelihood open your eyes to the fact that other Black parents live through them too. We're all real world people and there's no benefit in hiding the cold truth of this situation from ourselves. I'd prefer we face these facts with clear eyes and realistic expectations. I've found the frontal approach to be the best way to face the future, and deal with hard real life experiences.

Fact of Life Number One: African American young men are by nature inattentive and ungrateful.

They need to learn these graces over time, and with some assistance (reminding). I know parents get irritated with ungrateful or frightfully flakey sons! Be patient, he'll come around. Give him time.

Fact of Life Number Two: Life has a leveling action.

No matter how strange or bizarre or dysfunctional your son may seem at times to be, he will show at some time an equal amount of positive behavior. Now you might not be around to see it, but it will happen. Other parents will say "Your son is so nice and has such great manners. You will think "you've got the wrong one BABBY."

In science there is a concept called the law of averages. It suggests that there are average amounts of behavior that people are likely to do. There is an average amount of hair combing, an average amount of crying, and average amount of sweating, etc. Everything has an average.

The Law of Averages says that people will tend to hover around their personal average on any one behavior, and return to it quickly, if they deviate from the norm. Let's say there is an average amount of times you say each day, "I love you." If your average is 4 times per day, there is a high probability that you won't deviate from that average number. If you do, there is a high probability that you will return to your average *quickly.* If on one day you don't say it at all, there is a good chance the next day you will return to your average and say it 4 times. If one day you say it, 150 times, chances are good that on the next day, you will return to your average and say it 4 times.

If your African American young man does something really odd (and he will) you can expect normal behavior to follow. The problem may be that you will be too busy reeling backward about the bad stuff, to notice the good stuff! Very normal! Get your balance and start looking. Good usually follows bad, and bad usually follows good.

Fact of Life Number Three: There are few "meaningful" averages in behavior!

Is your African American young man average? Well, I hope so, but I must tell you that "average" happens over a suspiciously large area. Is there an average amount of crying African American young men do? Of course there is an average. Is it important or informative? *NO!* You might feel like you have a sense of what is normal and what isn't, and I would suggest you trust that feeling more than what you read. You will find that the most interesting aspects of your son are outside "the realm of averages." Can he love? Does he have a developing sense of character—right and wrong— fairness? Many things are beyond the artificial sensibility of statistical averages. Concern yourself not so much about, whether your African American young man is normal, but whether he is *exceptional.*

Fact of Life Number Four: Statistically speaking, 25 percent of all they do is extreme. Think about this word "extreme." If they do 100 things per day, 25 of them will be extreme *for your son.* It's as normal and predictable as the seasons. No matter how good little Junior was, a large chunk of his behavior had to be bad! African American young men cannot be good all the time it's impossible! Now, he can't be a complete outlaw either, nor, can he be a complete angel. He bounces around in between both with terrific predictability! Prepare for this ahead of time and save ourself some broken expectations!

Fact of Life Number Five: African American young men beg for direction and guidelines.

They ask for direction and guidance in strange ways. Research indicates that African American young men feel neglected if strict guidelines and performance standards *aren't* expected. It gives them a sense of security to know that there are external sources of final authority that have control. Relax the guidelines, and the African American young men will react by forcing you to re-enact more! African American young men are simply not happy "doing their own thing', "or being totally free." Give them what they are asking for!

Fact of Life Number Six: Identities will emerge that you don't know. Get ready for "Jekyll and Hyde." We reviewed the extent to, African American young men experiment with things. Personalities and identities are also included. Strange personalities will come and go. I suggest you let them float on through, for usually African American young men will end up embarrassed by them, dropping them like hot-potatoes, often times as fast as they put them on.

Fact of Life Number Seven: What's "well adjusted" changes with the wind. Have you watched daytime talk show television recently? I would urge you not to accept that what we are being told is normal as what really is good or normal! What we see on these shows is not everyday life. It's not *well adjusted* everyday life either.

The world's standard of what is "well adjusted" swings wildly around a fulcrum of social fadism. I've stated that 90-95 percent of Black males are perfectly normal and well adjusted. It is very normal and common for parents to hear about the latest "abnormal" things. The bad elements gain far too much press.

Do yourself a huge favor and invest in some original thinking about what you perceive to be well adjusted. I promise you that your definition will have more balance, depth and credibility than anything the world will offer you. Think for yourself and trust what you think.

Fact of Life Number Eight: Your Black male is going to break your heart. He's going to surprise you, he's going to run from you, he will spurn you in ways that will be very painful. I'll never forget the day I first saw this reality with my sons. It was the day we talked about sex. After the conversation, as I walked away, I knew that a certain part of my sons was gone forever.

I'm quite certain they won't tell me if they had sex. They're young men.

Do those things outlined in this plan and he will have a *foundation* from which he will never escape. Even though his behavior may shake and alarm you now, far off in the distant future one day he will thank-you for that base you built in hopeful faith.

Fact of Life Number Nine: Your African American young man didn't choose to be who he is.

I have a copy of Og Mandino's book *The Greatest Miracle in the World.* It's a timeless little book that is full of courage and love for the things in life that really count. The book talks about how each of us is the greatest miracle in the world.

Too often many children have never been told what a miracle they were. In all their uniqueness, in all their thoughts and dreams, they were a one of a kind. Many of them had never been talked to that way. They only knew they were one of a kind all-right!!! The bad seed.

Your African American young man is beginning to realize some things about himself that you have known for a long time. He was born with traits and qualities that will make life hard for him, but both of you can live with. You might deeply wish that life were different from the way it is. He might wish his life was different, as well. Either way, accept him, and commit to being the best father or mother you can be to him. He is the greatest miracle in the world!

Fact of Life Number Ten: "With my dying breath . . ."

Black males need constant reassurance of your love, support and endless forgiveness. Those qualities don't normally compute in a son's head, so they forget and need to be reminded often. Even when spoken often, African American young men still have a hard time believing them! Just love them; always support them and stand by them, and forgive without ceasing.

Fact of Life Number Eleven: Everything's gonna be alright!

Norman Cousins tells a great story in his book *Head First*. He tells of a time he was at a football game, and an emergency squad gathered around a guy lying on the ground, the victim of an apparent heart attack. The guy lay still, dazed and confused, and pale with fear. The emergency personnel were hustling around, proficiently doing their jobs, but Cousins noticed that *nobody* was talking to the man! He relates that at one point, all of the emergency people had walked away from this poor guy, for a minute, leaving him totally alone, wondering, Cousins surmised, whether he was going to live!

Cousins, acting on instinct, coolly strode up to this quivering fellow and placed his hand on the mans shoulder. He warmly looked the guy in the eye and said, "You know Mister, this emergency squad is the best I have ever seen. They are the most well trained and best equipped group you could have possibly gotten. They know exactly what they are doing, and you can rest assured that you are getting the finest care available. Everything's gonna be alright!"

Everything's gonna be alright. Lots of people have survived boyhood and so will you!

Action To Take: *You can begin now. This chapter has presented you with sufficient background to move forward. Let's look at the process of "how-to" develop the traits of African American men.*

▚ CHAPTER 9
To Be Young, Gifted and Black

When I discover who I am, I'll be free.

—Ralph Ellison

African American young men are not like us. They perceive situations and people differently, their understanding of power and social positioning is foreign to us, and they think at levels we've long since outgrown. These all combine to make understanding childhood joyfully impossible! But, you'll never have more fun, getting practically nowhere!

I'll ask you the question: Who understands African American young men better? The answer you give says a great deal about how you'll approach understanding your son. My mind says "science must have some answers," but my heart knows better.

How many different ways can we analyze African American young men? We could interview them, or I could create a list of qualities they possess, or we could read the newspaper or watch t.v. I have discovered that we can gather endless knowledge about African American young men, but *understanding* them is a radically different matter. Knowledge is, recognizing habits and tendencies, weak point, strong points, and other similar kinds of information. Understanding, however comes from firsthand insight into motives, knowing how all the pieces of information fit together, and having a feel for what it's like. You can *know* a lot about someone, yet never be close to *understanding* them.

Understanding African American young men must come from personal experience. Secretly, we're all anxious to grab for that wonderful youthful feeling. B.E.T. and African American movies clearly understand this. They tempt us with entertainment, movies, and ads that glorify the youth and the magic of being young again.

Isn't there something young inside each of us? Unfortunately, we spend too little time pursuing the simple types of joy we had as kids. Even though we all may wish away, childhood, always seems just slightly out of reach—just a little too far back in the past. We can never seem to recapture the real magic.

The best way to help raise your African American young man is to become a better Black man or Black woman yourself. You cannot learn it, so you must relive it. You can only understand after you have played in, that crazy universe called childhood, or by allowing yourself to really remember that far off time when anything was possible. You can walk a mile in his shoes by walking a mile in your own.

And what if you're a woman? Don't think your automatically dismissed. I don't think you can really know what being a African American young man was like, you certainly have enough experience with Black men who have not grown up to get the general idea. If you apply yourself to recreating the essence of childhood, you will be doing your son a remarkable favor.

In the early 1500's, Juan Ponce De Leon scoured the Caribbean looking for a fountain that the natives claimed, rejuvenated those who bathed in it. Your African American young man has found that "fountain of youth" and he bathes in it every day. You may join him if you choose. Becoming a young man again can form the foundation for a very special friendship.

Let's take two steps to learn about how African American young men think. First, let's have some fun with the following list. It's a short list of experiences you share in common with your son, but probably hadn't thought about. Find a quiet spot, read the list, item by item, and stop to let your mind drift after each. Just let your mind wander . . . that's what children do.

presents wrapped up with a bow

worms

hot summer days

pulling weeds

girls

ice cream

baseball games

funny looking people

girls

deserving to get chewed out

summer camps

girls

thunderstorms

dark basements

girls

noises at night
feeling like you got away with something
girls
suddenly alone in a strange place
five pieces of gum at once
a song that gets stuck in your head
girls
The smell of a fair
stepping in the muck at the bottom of a pond
snowball fights
girls
walking to school
your first grade classroom
Your favorite spot in your home
girls
Getting the neighbor mad at you
The safety of your mother's or father's arms
Grandma and Grandpa's house
Hanging out with the boys

I hope you have enjoyed this. Without further hints and suggestions, it's the best chance you have for really recalling much about your childhood. Your brain is strewn with thousands of memories such as these. Most of them are in shards and scraps, and so you don't remember them as well as you will recognize them. That is why with some prompting like this exercise, you can easily retrieve specific memories.

The Normal African American Young Men's Obsessions

As adults, we've rushed far away from the real texture of childhood. The effect of this movement make it harder and harder to relate with, what our kids are going through. We don't "get it" like they do, and we frankly are of little use to them if we remain insensitive to "how" they operate. Where there is no basis for commonality, vital connections between our sons and ourselves erode, and unity stops. Nobody wants to be an impotent parent particularly, if you have a commitment to be exceptional.

I want to give you some information that will help you think about how African American young men think. Listed are four major elements:

1. African American young men are sensory captive
2. African American young men are highly instinctual
3. Immense curiosity shortens attention spans to seconds
4. The world is black or white

By *sensory captive* I mean that African American young men live in a world confined to what they can see, hear, touch, smell and taste. This is very different from the way you operate. Until the onset of self-consciousness, they understand the world by looking, sniffing, grabbing, biting and poking. They are not thinking nearly as much as just collecting information. That's why it is important to provide the right information. Even after the transition, African American young men still tend to focus on body noises, squirmy animals, breaking glass; anything that excites the senses!

By *highly instinctual*, I mean that African American young men do not operate from a position of automatic logic (as we adults do) as much as by intuitive "feel." Where brain power is absent, instincts dominate. African American young men are very conscious of white people and events around them, but respond quickly to feelings of intimidation, power, pecking orders, and territoriality. Their instincts are not subject to thoughts like an adult, but are rather "built-in" defensive and offensive schemes that enable them to act in the world. This is one of the key reasons some African American young men can grow up more or less normal in the most adverse situations imaginable.

Curiosity

An African American young man's attention span is control-led by curiosity and is at the mercy of salient sensory stimulation. That's a Harvard way of saying you pay attention to the most noticeable things around you. Curiosity is the cognitive force behind short attention spans. African American young men must over time learn to ignore the extraneous activities going on around them and focus on one thing. Nature has wired them mentally to "latch on" to things that move, spark, dazzle, boom and bang. African American young men are controlled by these forces, and you as a seasoned and focused adult may be unable to appreciate their difficulty in channeling these forces.

Black and White

By black or white, I mean that African American young men only learn by experience that there are gradations between qualities such as: good and bad; right and wrong; love and hate. To them, life is an either or with no in betweens. For example, until African American young man reach the eight to ten year old range, they have a difficult time realizing that you can love them, and be mad at them at the same time. For a African American young man, those two cannot exist at the same time! Is it any wonder that so many black males run around feeling confused? We become more confused when white society uses such examples to label us:

White	or	Black
is		is
Right	or	Wrong
Good	or	Bad
Love	or	Hate

Using this chart, black is wrong, bad and hate are on one side. On the other hand white right, good, and love, are on the other.

Needs

What you are is equal to the sum total of all your yesterdays. All your experiences and thoughts combined, have brought you to this instant in time. To have arrived here with any degree of sanity, your parents or caretakers must have done something *right*. Whether you remember these right things, is immaterial. The fact remains that to be generally "normal" they had to have met some of your basic needs. If those people met those needs for you, you can then meet them for your son.

▦ CHAPTER 10
Wrestle-Relationships

*Children see things very well sometimes - and
idealists even better.*

—Lorraine Hansberry

African American young men communicate very little through verbal channels. Communicating with African American young men for understanding comes with the application of a different approach. Talk with your touch.

He Needs a Relationship

Your African American young man shares the same space in life that you do, but is completely unaware of the nature of the bond linking you. All he knows is that you are there, and he wants you to stay there. But he maintains a strange urge. His emotions are steering him to get close to you. He doesn't intellectually understand what's happening; he only knows that he wants physical closeness. This drive is responsible for many kinds of behavior that we as parents might otherwise think of as bothersome or unnecessary. Nuzzling, touching, sitting on your lap and holding hands are simple examples. To your son, they are life and death.

African American young men need to be touched. They will do almost anything to get touched. For them, it is the prime expression of love and attention, and without it they feel neglected and unloved. This force is built-in for good reason, and you must be alert to its presence.

African American young men constantly ask for physical contact. Because they don't know they need it, it's pointless to think that they could ever ask you for it. Their requests are non-verbal. They want you to put down the paper, and look at them when they speak. They want to hold hands and sit on your lap. They want hugs. They want you to sit next to them at the table. They want you to play with them and wrestle. They want to feel your arms around them. To your son, these moments are thousands of times more meaningful than thrown around "I love you's."

They want to give touches too. Think about this: Wouldn't it make sense that the best way they have to tell you they love you is through touch? For adults, relationships build and reinforce a deeper bond between two, unbonded people. Relationships are a two way street. If carefully nurtured, they build into a bond that is greater than the sum of the interaction between you.

African American young men feel naturally bonded to you, and their prime urge is to *express* the joy and sense of happiness they feel when they're around you. A parent/child relationship is the most special connection you can ever have with another human being.

Do you realize how blessed you are to have a son? He just wants to be close to you, and though he can't give you much else, his personal contact is the best he has to offer. There is a special way you can honor that effort: Return it.

How?

I have studied and puzzled over this relationship riddle for a long time. Relationships seem to be made up of pieces that fit together like a patchwork quilt. But I sense there's much more to it than just that. Relationships are more than just interactions with each other, no matter how bonded we are. Good relationships have what for lack of a better word is a "mystical" quality about them.

Can the special mystery of good relationships with sons be created on purpose? Of course, but it must happen unconventionally. Creating relationships that build powerful Black men depend on building good relationships, that little young men understand. Creating powerful Black men is always an ambitious undertaking. It won't happen by some space age technology, it won't happen through psychology, or drum beating or chemistry. The magic of the human connection can only occur between two people: You and your son.

The "how's" of an unconventional approach can be broken down into three steps. 1) gain rapport through playfulness; 2) challenge unspoken relational rules, and 3) reach out and touch him.

You need to be *inspired* to display your unique playful-ness. Think about this: Teaching is the introduction of new information, inspiration is bringing out the stuff that is *already inside you*. Learn this difference. Playfulness, fun-lovingness, joy, and light-heartedness must spring from within you! Those qualities are inside, no matter how drab you may be. Playfulness forms a special kind of rapport that builds a relationship of change.

I've Got a Secret

You just need to be willing to take the first step and roll-up your sleeves, let down your hair, and come play in the dirt. If you have a bullet-proof ego, you'll have a blast! Forget your psychological problems and get down here with us! Your African American young man will be surprised when he sees you on his level, and that's the start of some solid rapport.

Unspoken Rules

We obey unspoken rules. These rules not only apply in relationships with other people, but in all sorts of social settings. You know the "pressures" you feel to perform, to "do and not to do" certain things, in certain settings? For instance, among co-workers you might feel pressure to act, dress, or talk in a certain way that you wouldn't with a close friend. Nobody insists that you act, dress, or talk a certain way, but you feel as though if you don't . . . you're breaking a rule.

It's a strange thing, these rules. We voluntarily treat them as though they're etched in granite. They aren't, but they have this feeling that to violate them is to commit a serious crime. What's crucial is that inside relationships, clusters of rules exist. Churches, clubs, gangs, work, all have their unspoken rules. Your relationships are under the direct influence of secret forces you don't control! We obey these hidden rules by acting in ways you think the relationship demands that we act.

None of your relationships are "rule free." Rules bind and constrain every interaction you have with every other human being. For better or for worse.

The only way relationships among people grow and change is if the rules are challenged and changed. If unchallenged, these unspoken rules will over-control you right into stagnation and boredom. They have the ability to choke-off any kind of a relationships. The only way to change the relationship you have with others is to find out what the rules are and challenge them.

Effectively dealing with rules is at the heart of gaining rapport with African American young men. Every relationship has rules for gaining rapport. This means that for every person you do or don't know, there's a set pattern of words and actions you use to make contact with them. Nothing is stopping you from acting any way you choose, except the rules you choose to perform by.

What does this mean for you and your son? It means that better rapport between you can grow from challenging whatever rules you sense are stifling you. They need to be challenged. How?

When you feel like you must act a certain way with him, quickly do the opposite. If you feel like you must say "Good morning," you could challenge the rule by grabbing him and throwing him to the ground! That would be a delicate bend of the rule, no? Just impulsively react to the stifling rules when you feel them.

The things you do to challenge the flow are going to have a jarring effect on your African American young man. Jarring is usually good, and momentarily opens up vast new frontiers of friendship. Think about this: The moment you have challenged the rules, you can for a short moment do anything you want, because your action has *suspended* all the rules.

Don't make your bond with your son bondage for both. Use this as a rule of thumb: Be spontaneous at any instant you feel as though you are just plodding through the normal interactions with your kid. Just jump up and do something different . . . **anything!** within reason. This has the effect of bending and stretching—bringing forth a fresh flexibility into your bond.

Building Bridges

Diana Ross had a hit song called "Reach Out and Touch Somebody's Hand."

People touch in many ways. You've felt a "warm" glance from someone you love. You've felt a cold stare from someone who hates you. You've given reassuring smiles. You've been "tongue-lashed." You've given gentle encouragement with a kind voice. You've dealt harsh blows with a with a deadly glare and fiery squeeze of the hand. "Touching" someone is a remarkable jungle of activity and understanding.

Touchless Ways to Touch

You can see that you don't really have to actually touch someone in order to "touch" them. To learn the fine and delicate art of really touching someone, try a few of these. The selection is large, and the outcomes are fun. They serve the dual purpose of providing an implicit challenge to the rules of rapport you maintain. Have fun with this, and don't ever expect your son to give you back anything for your efforts. He'll just feel touched . . .

Stare at him without a word
Wear some cologne that he likes
Make him come and smell something you smell
Put a surprise somewhere and tell him where to find it
Put a friendly note in his lunch box
Buy him a funny card
Name a tree after him
Ask his opinion
Make him a special meal
Repeat his exact words after he speaks
Imitate him
Call him on the telephone

Send him a letter

Build him something with your hands

Put a post-it note on his tooth brush

Put out a totally mismatched set of clothes for him

Read a story to him

Put a name tag on his place at the dinner table

Put a "welcome home" banner on the house after school

Make up a song about him and sing it to him

Say a poem with his name in it

Draw a picture of you both doing something fun

Unplug the T.V. and tell him you are the entertainment for the
night

Split a large bag of M&M's with him right before dinner

Plant a flower bulb for him

Give him a day off school to be with you

Take him to work for the day

Throw an instant party in his honor

Write "I love you" on his hand in pen as they sleep

Buy him some cheap cologne that you like

Give him an autographed picture of you

Write messages on the windows with dry-erase markers

Write and publish a personals column to him

Leave a number where he can call you for fun

Call under false pretenses and really pull his leg

Sit and wait for him somewhere

Stop all you are doing and listen to him

Whisper across the room to him

This list can be as long as you are creative. What counts
is that each of these gestures will touch your son. Each touch
gives him substance, verifies his presence and value, and
makes him feel set apart and special. You are building a
relational foundation that will last forever.

Now You Need a Wrestle-Relationship

African American young men are *not* generally reserved or gentile beasts. Just look at their sneakers and pants for goodness sakes! Dirt and holes! They understand rough and tumble, and that is precisely how you should approach them.

I mentioned moments ago the terrific importance of touch, and the need for you to know the various ways to make physical contact. Allow me to make a short list:

Punch and poke
Pinch and grab
Hug and tickle
Kiss and twist
Pet and scratch
Hold hands and carry them
Wrestle and tussle

I suspect some elaboration is in order. Punch and poke gently! Pinch and grab quickly and at unexpected moments. Hug and tickle with no forewarning and with complete abandon! Kiss on the lips, twist the cheeks and ears. Pet them on the head, and scratch them on the back. Grab their self-conscious hands and swoop them full body up into your arms! Dive on the floor and mess up their hair! Do this all in happiness and love!

Most of you probably play like this with your sons anyway. Do it more. The benefits will build over time. If it's totally foreign to you, start slowly and build activities as you feel more comfortable. No need to rush, but be thinking about ways you might like to employ the list. If you've never done any of these things with your son, he might be a little annoyed at the whole proposition. I promise, though, that he will warm up to it quickly.

Remember, the point is to make contact that African American young men understand; a bridge by which your lives become verifiably connected. From that bridge build a relationship that expands into other areas of his life over the course of your mutual lifetimes. The only mistake you can makc is to make no attempt at all.

⊞ CHAPTER 11
Inch by Inch

Education is our passport to the future, for tomorrow belongs to the people who prepare for it today.

—*Malcolm X*

Building African American men takes time. I've observed an immutable law of the Universe that nothing of any value happens quickly. The slowness of the development has a distinct pattern. You surge forward; then have set-backs; then forward for a few more steps; then you reverse again. Life's forward/backward characteristic no one escapes. Your relationship with your son *will not be born* in one interaction. It *will not die* in one, or two that go bad. You can expect many victories and many defeats on this relational journey. The most painful experience you will ever have is feeling the excruciating crawl of time. It's slow, but it does heal and correct almost everything.

What you have is a start. You probably won't wrestle with your son when he's 50, but I promise you that when he is 50, he won't forget wrestling with you. Building great relationships begins now, and from scratch. You have the opportunity to begin building expectations that you will "mix it up" with him at any time. Today this means physically, but in the future, it will translate into working together on problems, and helping one another in your lives as you all grow old together. Keep in mind that most of your life will be spent with your son when he is an adult. You both are passing through his childhood now, but it's going to be over with very soon.

Wrestle while you may . . .

Why Won't this Kid Talk?

Get to the Point: *When you finally do get your African American young man to speak, the process can be very frustrating. You can learn a few tricks to open up your son quickly and communicate with clarity and understanding. To miss this lesson might be to miss some powerful opportunities to connect with your son.*

"I can't think when I'm itching" he replied, beginning to squirm.

Checkmate. I shut up and let him go. You've heard of chafing at the bit to get going? Wrong end, I'm afraid!

The Problem

The problem here is two-fold. The first fold is a tendency for African American young men to talk less to you as they get older, and to "clam-up" for strange reasons. This situation pressurizes quickly because you have a relentless need to converse with him. Parents are naturally curious about what their sons are thinking, and will turn any doorknob or pick any lock necessary to get inside.

The second arises from our need to ask clear questions, and the confusion inherent in all verbal communication. Don't make the mistake of thinking that what your African American young man has said is what he means. Most conversations are not what they appear to be, and you make literal interpretations of spoken words at the risk of massive error! Deciphering what African American young men mean—based on what they say—is very tricky, and the next chapter will detail how to handle this situation.

Open the Door

There are specific ingredients that will make him clam-up, and others that will make him open like a faucet. Let's first look at the mechanics of a "clam-up" to find insights for fixing the problem.

African American young men are unaware of how badly we seek to know them. Even though we learned in the last chapter how to relate through physical contact, what about *our* need to talk? As adults, we lean heavily on talking to communicate with others. Talking is something we're good at. It's practical and gets the message delivered quickly. We are so dependent upon talking, that when it wheezes and sputters to a stop with our African American young men we become immediately frustrated. We almost reactively begin to wonder, what he's hiding.

Adults are skillful at figuring out what people are hiding. We are all good "mind readers." We know from experience that people erect barriers to prevent us from knowing what they think. We all intuitively understand that people use their tongues more to hide information than to reveal. So, we employ tricks and methods to tease out that information we suspect lies hidden in others. Especially kids.

This really gets bizarre when you consider that adults and older children *know* they are playing these "hiding games." We spend a great deal of time playing this cat and mouse game. Guessing about what the other is not saying! "What does he really mean by that?" You might wonder or, "Is he really serious?" and "I think he's lying." We get pretty good at guessing. We have to because, *lying and hiding is part of the nature of people.*

African American young men can easily thwart every possible effort to get inside. We know that African American young men need to open up to grow; getting them to do so is another matter. African American young men have neither our facility with the language, or our ability to read and interpret what's hidden. The language we manage with such refinement, they stumble and bumble with. *Therefore, speaking with an adult is intimidating.*

The difficulties arising from this disparity can really pressurize a parent-child relationship. Because most kids don't *look* like they have any trouble expressing themselves. Don't be fooled; African American young men are very easily confused in conversation.

For now you must accept that the best conversation possible is only equal to the ability of the least conversant person. In most cases this will be your kid.

The Challenge

When our African American young men won't talk to us, we feel like it is an immediate personal rejection. "Butt-out!" we hear internally when junior says "I don't want to talk now." "You're too dumb to help me," is how we interpret him saying "just forget it." There are a variety of good reasons your son might clam-up, many having nothing to do with you. As your African American young man grows and changes, he naturally withdraws from the childlike naive openness of a two to six year old, to a cunning and selective way of interacting. He is not as inclined to share with you *all* that's going on. Like when he was younger. You'll now have more experiences of him "clamming up." This the first link in a chain of potential trouble.

The rest of the chain will develop quickly. Nobody likes feeling spurned by children, so you move to do something. You turn down the screws, turn up the heat, cajole, laugh and pat him on the back, or cattle prod him to get more information. He doesn't answer, seems to become more stubborn, so you erupt. I call this set of problems, "The Shootout," and it's a classic pattern in many homes.

The prime reason African American young men clam-up is what psychologists call "demand characteristics." Demand characteristics are the unspoken expectations and pressures African American young men sense in social situations that they believe demand how they are to behave. We all are constantly bombarded with racism, and our brains are tuned to find them, accurately interpret them and act in response.

African American young men are hyper-alert to these cues, and they apply riveting attention to figure out what's expected. Noticing these pressures and responding to the expectations is important to African American young men because they want to please adults. If an African American young man feels for any reason that he doesn't or can't understand what's expected of him in a situation, he'll become quiet and just watch.

Not knowing this, you as a well meaning parent turn up the pressure to pry out information. Do you see how that could happen? You ask more questions at a faster pace, hoping desperately for a response. This changes the atmosphere of the conversation. The pitch and volume of your voice shifts and your looks become more intense. None of these changes get past the ever sharpening instincts of your son. Frustration displays itself as anger in the ears of a African American young man. He hasn't the slightest idea how to handle the deteriorating situation, so he does what's natural: He squirms and fidgets and tries to get away. To your eyes this looks like loathsome obstinacy.

The problem can become much more serious than this.

You can, over the course of time become frustrated and embittered, perhaps even giving up on your son. He can feel perplexed at what he sees as unmerited rejection. Over the course of a few difficult interactions, the entire relationship can descend. Nothing moves forward, communication dissolves, and a bad habit gets seeded.

This pattern cycles daily to greater or lesser degree in most homes, yours included. You press, he resists, and your whole world seizes. Let's look at how to create a win-win situation and avoid habitual clam-ups.

How Do Expert Communicators Do It?

What are these communicators doing? Four distinct activities:

1. They are aggressive listeners
2. They are sensitive to incongruency
3. They use active language and ideas
4. They don't push conversations, they attract them

1) Eyes Tell No Lies

It's common for African American young men in this situation to ask "what's wrong with you!" Why? For starters, they simply aren't used to having someone pay aggressive attention to what they are saying. Furthermore, many African American young men aren't familiar with having someone really try to understand what they are saying!

Active listening encourages listeners to make good eye contact, nod their heads occasionally, and make appropriate sounds ("uh huh," "hmmmm," "oh my!," etc.). This was all very commendable, because for the first time people could successfully model actions of naturally gifted communicators. Best of all, the speaker felt listened to, proving remarkably therapeutic.

Excellent communicators take this whole idea and turn the intensity up a few clicks. They do more than just listen and respond, they look carefully at the child and intensely focus on not only what's said, but how it's said. They offer penetrating response to statements by thinking carefully about words, context, and logic. Your son could greatly benefit from this energetic focus and thoughtfulness from you.

2) Sensitivity to Incongruency

An incongruency is a sophisticated and unconscious "double message" in your speaking. Like: saying that you love your dog while you're shaking your head meaning "no."; Telling your boss you can make that sale, while you are quivering and beginning to sweat; Telling someone that you want to be near them as you snicker and back away! These are all examples of behaviors that don't match or mesh with your words. They are incongruent. Speakers are usually unaware of the mismatches, but a sharp aggressive listener can detect them with little difficulty.

We frequently commit these incongruencies in our conversations with others. We don't do it on purpose; incongruencies are the result of normal unchecked internal confusion that we all experience and have learned to live with. The most obvious question for a listener when we notice them is "which one do I believe, what I hear or what I see?"

Master communicators are crafty in observing and challenging incongruencies within children. Their flare is initiating conversation without creating defensiveness. Their conversational magic allows them to hurdle the apparent conflict while making the child feel understood and respected.

3) They Use Active Language and Interesting Ideas

Master communicators have a good command of language. They use active words and colorful expressions. I have no trouble getting kids to talk with me because I show real concern for them. This kind of interaction is easy and entertaining for African American young men to participate in. Perhaps you know people who are tastefully dramatic in their use of inflections, tones, and cute words. If the language used is unusual, you can bet a child will notice.

Interesting ideas grab attention. If you ask any African American young man if they have any good CD's (music), they will stop—guaranteed—and tell you about their music. The use of right words, increases the chance that they will respond to you. Expert communicators use these sorts of interesting and strange ideas to arrest the attention of listeners, long enough to engage them in conversation.

4) They Don't Push Conversations, They Attract Them

Using the assortment of talents listed here, these master communicators find themselves extracting conversations out of African American young men, rather than constantly having to force the dialogue. African American young men find these people intriguing and fun to talk with. African American young men will seek these people out!

To become a master, you must find a few of the following techniques that suit you well and apply them daily. The targeted talents of the masters we've described (being an aggressive listener, sensitivity to incongruence, using active language/ideas, and attracting conversation) will grow as your application becomes your personal habit.

Change Your Expectations

Your expectations can create pressure in your life and in the lives of those around you. Without being aware, you telegraph to those around you, hints about what you expect from them. Often African American young men respond with hesitation and defensiveness, launching the classic clam-up.

Expectations are a complex signaling system necessary for a happy life. That might strike you as a strange statement, but consider for example that an experience cannot satisfy or disappoint you until you make an internal comparison about what you expected. You cannot, for instance, know that it's time to feel "good" or "bad" about something without first making a quick mental comparison against what you expected. That's how you know if what happened to you is something you liked or didn't like.

If your son is acting like a total jerk, and you expect that, your life will continue on unchanged. If on the other hand, you expect your son to be gracious and thoughtful, and then he acts jerky, your expectations signal you that it's time to be upset. *Your expectations "set the dial" for evaluating what's happening to you in all situations.*

You must first find out what you expect from your conversation with your son. This is simple to do with a little thought, and some writing. Write down your expectations in a narrative form. Start by thinking about that last talk you had with your son. What did you expect to get out of the talk? How did you really expect your son to respond? Did he do what you thought he would do? What sort of reaction did that get from you?

If you answer these questions with brief replies you will find patterns of expectations that influence all your parent/son conversations. It may also tip you to what specific expectations trigger which attitudes from within the confines of your dialogues.

There are infinite varieties of emotional atmospheres around us at all times. We don't notice them because we are *in them*. Yet, they exert a strong control over what we feel and how we act. The most important thing to remember is that these atmospheres can actually become part of specific, or actual locations. For example: you walk in the kitchen and feel like eating; walk into your bedroom and feel like laying down; walk into your sons' bedroom and feel like leaving!

You must assume responsibility for an *effective talking atmosphere*. Do this: When difficulty emerges in talking with your son, feel absolutely free to change the venue. Go for a walk. Take a drive. Change shirts. Chew gum. Do anything! Just assume responsibility for changing the atmosphere from pressure and stagnation to something different.

Find Your Son's "Hot Buttons"

Do you have any topic that just really turns you on? Cars, Sports, Money? Well, so does your son. All the African American young men in our neighborhood are into basketball, cars, and honey hunting. These items pepper their conversations, and provide the fodder of endless chatter.

Everybody is orbiting around issues of personal interest. Each persons orbit has distinct features, "hot buttons," which you will notice if you observe a little. Your African American young man's "hot buttons" may not be of great interest to you, but you needn't like *his* interests to use them as fulcrum upon which to lever conversations. You just need to spend twenty minutes to familiarize yourself with those things he finds important and interesting. That's all it takes to become adequately familiar with a topic. Find twenty minutes and make a great investment in your sons future.

If you don't know your sons hot button, ask him! Make yourself do this. You might be surprised to find that what you thought he liked, he doesn't care for.

Talk Specifically About Interesting Things

For African American young men (and some of us) it's easier to talk about a "chair" than it is to talk about "happiness." You can connect with "football" much easier than you can connect with "self-control." Notice the concrete, touchable characteristic of some things, and the abstract, misty quality of others?

African American young men don't get the misty stuff. To have a good talk with your son you must have skill at speaking in concrete terms, about concrete topics. Adults get wrapped up in abstractions, so you need to make a pointed effort to keep your talk centered on solid and touchable topics.

Make yourself alert for one new and interesting topic each day. There are many of these topics floating around. Sources could be the newspaper (talk about fires, politics, wars in other countries, etc.), strange job experiences, or other peoples weird stories! Train your ears to listen for these oddities. It doesn't matter where they come from! Just keep your ears open, and you will find them!

"We have Ways to Make You Talk"

Don't intimidate your son on purpose. The African American young men don't like it. Sometimes the most effective thing you can do to pierce the shield of silence is to just back off. There are many parents around who routinely apply scare tactics to their kids. They threaten and physically intimidate them, thinking they can force conversation. This is uncalled for and should be stopped the instant you notice it.

If or when, you find yourself frightening or threatening your African American young man because he won't talk, just think:

If your pressure hasn't worked up to this point to create conversation, why would *more* pressure work? These are the moments to put away your thunder, and start listening.

Bullying parents need to learn some finesse. Learn some tact and treat your son like the magnificent creature he is. Make yourself become patient with people, make yourself kind to others when you would prefer to scream, keep your cool when everyone else is losing theirs, and be the calming source of stability when a war is raging around you.

Chill Out

You need to learn to give your African American young man time to think before you begin to demand answers. Everyone has a unique metabolism, cycle, period and speed, which controls various aspects of their lives. Thinking has its own cycle, and it's fast for some and aggravatingly slow for others. African American young men seem on average, to be slower in responding to adult generated questions than other adults are. Be patient with them and give them time to respond.

Feel free to encourage your African American young man to take his time in answering your inquiries. Minutes, hours or days if necessary. There usually is no particular rush to get an answer, so chill out and let him know you would rather have a good answer, than a fast one.

By way of practical suggestion, write down the exact verbiage of your question if you aren't going to expect an answer within a few minutes. This serves a dual purpose of reminding you to follow up and get an answer; and it permits you to know exactly what you asked. You will forget, and specific wording is crucial in understanding specific responses.

Action to Take: *Class is over. It's time to get to work. Simply select two or three of these items and apply them today. You shouldn't wait till an emergency arises to get proficient with them, and a little focused practice would be of marvelous benefit. Enjoy!*

▦ CHAPTER 12
That's a Great Question!

No race can prosper till it learns that there is as much dignity in tilling a field as in writing a poem.

—Booker T. Washington

The Art of the Question

Questions are one of the most versatile inventions of man. The Africans used questions for everything. They thought asking questions was an art form, and used them for teaching, inquiring and solving problems.

Now let me tell you about the "very pathetic" method I see many parents using! Most parents just don't ask questions, opting instead, to lecture their sons. African American young men need to be asked questions. Good questions which prompt thinking, pose new possibilities, and promote all aspects mental development.

"What do you want to be?"
"Would you ever rob a store?"
"Can you imagine building a machine that could. . . ?"
"What am I hiding in my hand?

Well formed, clear questions teach, illuminate ideas, encourage ordered thinking and reward us with clear answers. Master the art of the question, and you master a source of great power.

Questions fall into two broad categories: 1) clarifying what was said, and 2) eliciting information or response from others.

1) Clarification

You should never . . . NEVER believe that what you heard your African American young man say is exactly what he meant. It's impossible for them to utter exactly what they mean, let alone, understanding it. Why? It's a bit unorthodox to discuss this, but there are natural forces at work to derail our best efforts to communicate clearly. At best, what's spoken is only a rough representation of what our young men mean, and should be treated as such.

2) Eliciting Information

Brilliant conversationalists will tell you they aren't that brilliant. They understand that people love to talk about themselves, so they just *ask their listeners lots of questions*. It's

the listener that *thinks* they are brilliant! Such brilliant conversationalists have mastered the art form of asking questions for information and responses. Whatever brilliance they
possess is in the intuitive realization that questions have the
power to make things happen.

Questions used properly can persuade, gather information,
plant ideas, clear up thinking, motivate, problem solve,
overcome objections, gain cooperation, take the bite out of
criticism, or defuse explosive situations. You can get these
effects quite easily.

Inquiry type questions are typically "open" or "closed."
Closed questions are those that elicit a yes/no response.

"Are you sick?"
"Do you want to go to the movies?"
"Would you give me a million dollars?"

They are great for gathering simple and quick information,
but usually don't reveal substantial information. When possible, closed questions need to be changed to "open" questions.

Open questions allow elaborate answers. Any question
you could possibly ask could be opened with one of these
three lead-offs: What, How, or Could. These lead-offs encourage responses in the most pressure free way. When
asked questions of this sort, African American young men
are practically "led by the hand" to find new answers and to
elaborate on previously stated positions.

I want you to commit this list of questions to memory. They
are all questions of the "What-How-Could," variety and will
be very useful in drawing information out of your son.

What can I do to help?

What has to be done?
Could you explain a little more?
How does that make you feel?
Could you tell me what your reason is for asking?
What needs to change?
What are you trying to accomplish?
How can I talk to you so you will want to talk to me?

What do you want?
What's happening now?
What stops you from getting what you want?
What do you need to get your goal?
How will you know if you're moving toward your goal?
Have you ever had this happen before?

Any question you want to ask can be turned into a creative "What-How-Could" question. Questions like these can lead to good and useful answers. They work almost like magic, so apply them liberally and creatively. You can get any information you want if you pose the question properly. A little experimentation with this is all you need to give you a taste of real success. You can't make any mistakes, so try.

"Why" questions are dead-ends

Asking "why?" will usually get a conversation stuck. "Why?" is so common, and so human. It's also a very demanding question that will invariably create defensiveness and confusion:

"Why are looking at me like that?"
"Why did you say that?"
"Why are you such a little jerk?
"Why are you always trying to create trouble?"
"Why do you let those kids beat up on you?"

Do you sense the pressure, the urgency? Why questions are demanding on everyone, and African American young men will typically respond to that pressure by freezing.

The beauty of "What-How-Could" questions is that they suggest a new way to think. They pose inquiry, in a form that can be answered. They retrieve "why?" information in a much more sensible and non-threatening form.

"Why" questions usually pop-up during situations of duress. "Why did you do that?" or "Why do you always ignore me!" and so on. These questions quickly put listeners on the defensive. They do nothing to gain information, and usually serve the limited purpose of letting your son know you are mad or disappointed. Those are the moments to ask different questions.

Transform your "why" questions, and avoid the stress of a grinding halt in communication. "Why" questions can be reframed in the "What-How-Could" form and made more effective. Be creative. Don't ask me why!

Curiosity

Let's suppose for a moment that I were to give you a small laptop computer that learned by itself, and collected data and information on its own. Even though it would be slow at first, ask some dumb questions and make simple mistakes, it would learn. Later, it would pick up speed and really fly, eventually knowing too much for its own good! There is only one thing you must, absolutely must give it: Experience. Just give it experience and it does the rest.

This little computer would be the most mind blowing piece of equipment ever made. Nothing ever created could come close to it's performance specs. Well surprise! You've got one of those computers at home and he has arms and legs! By design he's motivated to take measure of the world and figure out the best path of growth. The only sustenance you need to provide him are experiences. He can do all the rest.

Think of curiosity as having a life, an entity of its own inside your son. It's very active and your son can't control it well. I suspect as boy raisers we look upon qualities such as curiosity as "being" our son, rather than being a *quality* that our sons possesses. Your son isn't curious, he *has* curiosity.

Remember two crucial facts: 1) curiosity is an independently operating entity inside your son; and 2) when it's operating, your son has a special look that you can learn to recognize and exploit. When curiosity shows itself you can grab the opportunity to feed it. Nourish it as often as you spot it, with experiences, questions, challenges, puzzles, odd facts, and lots of encouragement.

Now pay attention for the following public service announcement: *Curiosity may present itself to you as an irritant, causing you to be blinded to its presence.* It can disguise itself in your son and look like thoughtless actions, obsessiveness, and even downright stupidity. You might even think your son is mentally troubled. These reasons explain why childhood curiosity is so often foolishly squished.

As adults we are notoriously intolerant of recurring problems. I don't think you should let your son's curiosity run totally rampant, for that could be dangerous. But it's equally dangerous to pulverize it for the sake of making your life easier. A little discomfort isn't going to hurt you, so let your sons curiosity have a little more leash than he's had in the past.

Imagination: Everyone Is Schizophrenic

If you could secretly peer into anyone's mind during the day and see what they were thinking, you would swear they were psychotic. It's a bizarre tangle of strange thoughts, secret wishes, arguments, lies, and screams. What do we all look like on the outside? Smooth and unruffled, controlled and serene! An amazing contrast, don't you think?

Our brains epitomize reckless imagination and uncontrolled curiosity. We keep a tight lid on the whole machine, though so nobody knows what's occurring in here! The light bulbs unconsciously "ping" with ideas and schemes. Fantasies launch dreams; dreams feed desires. It's automatic complete madness.

The only difference between you and the people in the hospital, is that you control your imagination. Sometimes we control ourselves so much that we overcontrol, practically shutting off our idea-maker.

The prime difference between African American young men and adults is that African American young men are less disciplined in controlling their imagination. Imagination, to run fast and well, needs a "track" upon which to concentrate its energy. It must be harnessed and focused. For an African American young man to have a fully functioning imagination, there are two requirements: First, he must be disciplined enough to control his thought processes; and second, he must have a simultaneous ability to let it "run wild."

Imagination without control creates problems. African American young men with unruly imaginations usually have unruly energies. Unbridled energies can be very disruptive to both the young man and his family and friends. And, uncontrolled imagination is not natural. Kids learn to suppress themselves as they mature, and if not coached differently, they will be unable to maintain the imaginational savvy of a brightly thinking child into adulthood. Only disciplined practice will help imagination remain pliant and useful as African American young men grow older.

Your Habits

You've taught your son some habits that keep him from being so pitiful. Were you taught any habits by your parents? Are there any you wish they had insisted upon, but didn't? How would your life be different if you had better habits?

These are eye-opening questions! Imagine if you had learned better discipline, more stick-to-it-tiveness, more promptness, more decisiveness, and better physical condition. Would life be different for you? Now, try this: Imagine having *less* of any good habit you have now! That's a scary thought!

This contrast lets you feel the utter dependence your life today has on your current collection of habits. For better or worse, every day leaps from a recipe called "your personal habits." From the side of the bed you get up on, to the way you brush your teeth, to the way you drive to work, to way you drive home from work, to the way you schedule your evening, to getting back in bed. . . How much is just a pure routine, unnoticed habit?

Habits are simple, thoughtless behaviors. We are utterly dependent upon them to carry out countless measures of daily chores. Our brain creates them as often as possible to ease the amount work it has to do. Our brains easily turn actions into habits.

A Great Habit = Good Reasons + Good Reinforcers + Good Repetition

If we understand habits from an engineering perspective, we can learn how to build them good and strong. To accomplish this, we must search for the positive benefits habits create.

Such as: Smoking makes some people feel relaxed; brushing your hair makes people think you're attractive; procrastination gives you more time to avoid the discomfort of making a decision. Sharp analysis can reveal that habits have a good reason for being in operation.

Habits generate "strokes" or rewards that you like. That's what keeps them happening, even if the habit, like smoking is bad over the long term. According to our brains' natural law of economy, a habit needs to produce something positive and immediate or it won't become a habit in the first place.

Though some behaviors provide a positive benefit, they don't become habits. Your brain is pretty smart, and it requires *repetition* for a behavior to be automated into a habit. How many reps? It varies. Crack cocaine becomes a habit in about 10 minutes. Something without such a potent physical presence, like flossing your teeth takes daily exposure for twenty-one days. The key is repetition, plain and simple.

I'm not going to spend time explaining the details of making a new habit. Don't look for any magic because there is none. To create a habit, simply make sure your son knows the reason a habit is being created, reinforce his habit behavior with an acknowledgement when he does what he's supposed to do, and make him repeat the behavior with heartless consistency!

Habit formation is relatively lo-tech. It just makes simple sense, and there is no need to over analyze it or over coach you. Nature has organized your son to continually seek behaviors that are helpful, and self-generated rewards makes those behaviors thoughtlessly automatic.

I would make three suggestions: First, the level of difficulty in creating habits in African American young men increases with time. Like almost any other aspect of learning, the younger a child is when he first learns something the quicker it's picked up and the longer it stays. Once African American young men cross that thin line into self-consciousness, so many other factors enter into the mental mixture that the difficulty of learning new habits escalates steeply. Start them early.

Second, recall from an earlier discussion the importance of consistent models. African American young men pick up habits from adults and peer models with frightening ease. The last thing any child needs is two significant adults arguing over the propriety of one habit or another. It's very confusing. This problem usually crops up over habits of health like eating, exercise, alcohol, drugs and tobacco. As I mentioned earlier, do your best to align the habits of the people with which your son has contact. You will do him a great favor by making the effort to have all the adults in his life present a unified front. It reduces his confusion, and dramatically improves the chances of him adopting healthy habits he needs.

Third, the biggest problem you face in building habits is not actually creating habits, but in deciding what is a good habit for you son and what is not.

Good and Bad Habits

If you had been raised independent of any outside forces (like schools, churches, parents and teachers), your habits and your life would have followed a jagged line of least resistance. Your habits would have formed along the lines of your "comfort zone" wherever that happened to be. You'd still have just as many habits as you do now, but for radically different reasons. Your life would be very different than it is today.

Why isn't your life directed by every whim and pleasure? Because, you have developed a different, more disciplined group of habits that force your life to a higher level. Those habits deny you a little instant pleasure now in exchange for the promise of a lot more in the future.

We call these "good" habits. They force you to do things you wouldn't do naturally. Good habits align with prevailing standards of success, propriety, efficiency, class, good taste, and sociability. Examples might include proper speech, deference to authorities, politeness in the presence of strangers, and attention to detail. These habits have hopefully served you well, but how far could you have gone with a *better* list of habits?

Give Him what You Wished You Had

Wouldn't you love to give the habits you lack to your son? You are in a perfect position to judge what those missing habits are. Better personal habits will help your African American young man reach the top for at least three reasons. First, most of the good achievements in life require more than accidental effort. They require disciplined effort. That means the ability to make yourself do something you would rather not do. Disciplined effort is uncomfortable, but African American young men need to learn it.

Second, a disciplined African American young man with good personal habits stands out in the crowd. He can be his best, and has the means to be in a class by himself. Who wouldn't want this for their son? Don't miss this chance!

Third, having good personal habits makes learning the rest of the African American traits much easier. All the personal traits of African American men hang together and interact like a complex mental scaffolding. Good habits create their own internal support network, pushing the scaffolding skyward. Good habits push your life upward *whether you intend on it or not.* Even in situations when your focused efforts fade or dissolve.

By setting high standards for African American young men and making those standards habit, excellence can become "automatic" for them too. Certain habits form a volcanic catalyst in your son's life. Though he may not realize it, he too can be endowed with a style of acting that brings successful results.

Take this Habit and Shove It

Manners

Black men must be well mannered. I would suggest the creation of four specific habits with respect to manners: personal greetings, conducting introductions, table manners and phone manners.

These manners are simple to teach, and are forever useful to your African American young men. Personal greetings are a terrific example. Show your son how to shake hands, look people straight in the eye and say, "How do you do?" Simple. I work particularly hard on volume of voice and strength of the grip. "Squeeze the hand you are shaking and talk *loud.*" Practice this everyday. I've found the African American young men to catch on to this quickly and enjoy the confidence and control it makes them feel.

Table manners aren't so cut and dried. I know that all families have their routines around the table, and I don't want to tamper with your traditions. Just make sure you have some, for kids need predictability in their lives and this is one place where it is easy to apply. I would suggest that the family eats at least one meal a day together, for eating as a group has a timeless message. Historically the table has been the place that families have gathered to talk, share experiences, discuss problems and share some "down time" together. It's not asking too much to ask the kids to turn off the T.V. during meals, don't take phone calls, stay at the table till everyone's finished, use eating utensils (properly), thank God for the food, and the time shared together.

Phone manners are just as easily taught as table manners. Speaking loudly and firmly, saying "please" and "thank-you," taking good messages and repeating phone numbers are just a few suggestions. Be mindful of them and take the opportunities that arise to teach, correct, and encourage.

Today, it is practically impossible to get away with poor communication skills of any kind. Poor communication skills are one of the leading causes of people not advancing in jobs and careers. I strongly suggest that you set aside time to develop good habits on the telephone.

Chivalry

Get your sons in gear for *building habits of courtesy, bravery, and helpfulness.* How can you do this? Of the zones in which we build habits, this is the one that requires the most modeling. You not only need a plan for the creation of these qualities, but African American young men need physical models, showing how to do these skills. The model is you!

Courtesy is taught by instruction and repetition. Who should they be courteous to? Everyone. "Please" and "thank-you" are quiet acceptable. "Yes sir" and "no sir," "yes ma'am" and "no ma'am" are the standards of excellence. In addition to teaching them what to say, instruct them on the proper time to apply courtesy.

When you speak with this sort of deference and respect, you're treated differently than everyone else. Because it's so unusual, your son can quickly cut the lines of stereotypes to those with whom he speaks. It's a simple habit to teach. Run through the wordage a few times, model it for them, before they meet people, and ask that they in turn talk this way.

Helpfulness is different from everyday heroism. *Helpfulness is something you find to do around the house.* It doesn't take a genius to spot when someone around the house is in trouble, then jump to help! Yet, how many of us have struggled with grocery bags at the front door, while the kids sit and watch television, or have a phone go unanswered because nobody will get it?

Helpfulness is a tough habit to build because you want your son to have a *desire* to help. You want it to spring naturally from within your African American young man, not by twisting his arm. There are several ways this can be accomplished, but some are easier than others. Let me suggest two approaches.

First, tell them what you expect. Most kids that are by nature "unhelpful" and have never had their parents clearly explain what they expect from them. Remember that most sons are not aware of much anyway, let alone when to jump up and be helpful. Tell them clearly what you expect, and ask them to look for those moments and opportunities to pitch in and be helpful.

Secondly, build within them smaller qualities that add up to helpful behavior. Think of helpfulness as the combination of many other smaller habits, attentiveness to what's going on around them, appreciation for other peoples needs, sensitivity about family rules, and an appreciation that sometimes life is chaotic and everyone needs to help. Build on each of these qualities individually in little ways in real life experiences. Let those experiences, become his instructor. The combined weight of these individual qualities will make the probability of spontaneous helpfulness much greater.

Treating Women Properly

This might not appear to be "habit making" material, but during this age, African American young men need to learn important habits of interacting with young women. Parental attitudes at home, school experiences and neighborhood friendships form the interactive elements of this habit.

Interestingly, African American young men seem to need enemies. They need people to team up against, to fight against, to unite in opposition to, and so forth. Young women can appear to be natural adversaries. Sometimes, they look different, typically are more academically inclined as a group, mature faster, and often gain what is perceived to be preferential treatment from adults.

How can we encourage sons to treat our daughters properly? I would suggest a number of things. First, appreciate that you are laying the groundwork for something that might not necessarily show up immediately. All habits (especially those relating to treating women properly) are learned slowly, and must be massaged deeply into the life of your son. Set your expectations on a long-term, consistent and daily effort.

Secondly, teach your son to interact properly with his mother. Rehearse treating his mother with deference and respect, learn the fine unboylike qualities of touching gently and complimenting. Mom will love it.

Thirdly, build the habit of self control over his tongue. Specifically, no verbal abuse, foul language or reference to physical abnormalities. It is easy to be quiet, and often it is the best behavior an African American young man can do when he is around young women. The old "if you can't say something nice, don't say anything" message applies nicely here.

Fourthly, when your African American young man goofs up and is unnecessarily rude to a young woman, make him apologize. Make him. I've been very surprised in many conversations with young men to discover, the number of young men who agree they deserve to make restitutions or apologies for mistakes they've made!

Fifth, explain to your son what *you* expect. You don't need *me* to tell *you* exactly how to make your son conduct himself with young women. You have your own opinion, but perhaps you need to underscore them. I have offered a few ideas here, but the bottom line is you must decide what standards you want your son to perform. Then make it a goal for him to attain. Write it out, draw pictures, rehearse, do whatever you like. Provide precise definition and clear direction.

In most cases, African American young men have clear ideas of how to treat young women, but due to high concentrations of peer pressure, they buckle and act in a way contrary to their own beliefs. Encourage and persuade him to stand by his values and do what he knows is best. African American young men need the vote of confidence and persuasion from an adult. Especially about those things he feels deeply, but is embarrassed to admit in public.

Let's talk about money. Let's talk specifically about the difference in money the African American young men *get* and the money the African American young men *earn* . . . Money the young men often get is called an allowance. Allowances can create trouble in families. Allowances can be given for many good reason, but how much and for what effort is open to debate. I know parents who have developed elaborate point systems with reward and cash bonuses. Then again, I've seen homes doling out *double digit allowances on a weekly basis for nothing*! I grew up in a home with no allowance.

Allowances work best when they model something in the real world. If in the real world you work for cash, do so at home. If in your real world, you get money for nothing other than smiling, than do the same thing at home. Households that dole out money based on "waking up," risk what the government has discovered about entitlement programs: If you don't work to get it, you won't appreciate it or work to get more. Make certain that allowances reflect real life.

Now, let's talk about earning money. This is of course related to work, and it should be. Entrepreneurial ventures and hard physical labor should always be encouraged in your son. Be sure to teach that value of "making " money versus "getting" money.

Get your son to start something. Start a business or go and get a real job. Most of the businesses he will start will either be of the labor variety or the sales variety. Labor jobs include: paper routes, shoveling snow, raking leaves, mowing lawns, or chasing rabbits out of peoples gardens. Earlier I mentioned how many things other people would let you do if you just ask. It's equally amazing what people will pay little kids to do. Just encourage you son to ask for the job.

While on the topic of paid physical labor, it seems sensible to me to encourage your son to learn a wage earning vocational skill. Granted, this age might be a bit young to teach your kid to weld or pour cement, but having a wage earning vocational skill will enable him to always find work so he will never go hungry. Throughout his life he'll always be able to get a job doing his skill for real money. Teaching him these skills might be equivalent to feeding him for years into the future.

Sales jobs are a little different. Get him involved in a Junior Achievement group where he can learn all sorts of ways to sell products. If he just doesn't think he can sell, give him a copy of *The Greatest Salesman in the World* by Og Mandino. Just encourage him to jump in and try selling *anything*. He can only win.

When I discuss ownership, I'm referring to issues of responsibility with things and respecting personal property. If he works and puts forth some effort, he will accumulate money which inevitably translates into personal junk. Much like teaching him to care for his clothing. Go the extra mile to make him personally responsible for caring for his toys, bikes, radios and so on. Our society encourages disposability, no matter how alive the ecological movement remains. We are a society overbuilt on the foundation of convenience and "throw it away if it breaks." Do your son a favor and teach him the proper care of "things," and the value of *restoration*.

There are rewards for teaching your son to fix things that are broken, and not giving up on items of value if time or hard wear has left them damaged. I earnestly believe that sons taught to fix things treat *themselves* differently than sons who just pitch the broken or unwanted objects cluttering their lives. Imagine implanting within your son the sense of value that only comes when he can restore something broken! It's a skill that he will fall back upon even if his life shatters about him.

I've encouraged every African American young man I know to learn how to fix things. Flat footballs (which usually end up in the garbage can) can be fixed by tearing off the laces, pulling out the bladder, patching it with glue, replacing it and pumping it up. A flower that gets knocked over and smashed can be propped up with a stave, watered and nursed. Little birds with broken wings can be splinted and helped. I have a rule that I live by: "If it can be torn apart, it can be restored."

Also, encourage your son to make good and prompt decisions. The roots of procrastination grow deeply during youth, primarily because sons are allowed put off making decisions. Making decisions can be fearful, which in turn creates hesitation. The habit of decisiveness allows your son to experience how easy making choices can be. Start this habit by simply insisting that he choose between two things. Ask him to make a choice concerning two easy options. What does he want for dinner, meat or non-meat? Don't let him off the hook with an "I don't care." Where does he want to sit in the car, in the front or the back? How would he like his clothes folded, in halves or in quarters? This list could be endless. Just bear in mind that you want him to make quick choices between two simple options.

Be the Best

You have heard me echo the theme of "Be the Best," so let me just mention this: Your boy is more moldable and changeable today than he will ever be for the rest of his life. He's watching you. He's modeling you. Do you want him to be like you in every detail, good and bad?

If not, take this challenge to push yourself up a notch on the class and self-discipline scales. This reminds me of a story I heard: An aid to Henry Kissinger was asked to create a report and present it on a developing global situation. This aid went away, and returned the next week with a report packaged in a nice folder. After a day, Dr. Kissinger called the aid back and asked if that was the best he could do. The aid, being a little intimidated, responded that he thought he could improve it.

A week later the aid delivered an updated report. Once again after a day, Kissinger returned the report with instructions to improve it. The aid pulled out all the stops and created a beautiful report with more graphics and a more detailed analysis. After he delivered it again, he was again asked if it was the best he could do. The aid was completely exasperated. One last time he focused, polished, and groomed the report to a higher quality. It was the best he could possibly do. He had no more to give. He personally took the report into Kissinger and said, "Dr. Kissinger, you've asked me to revise this report many times. Each time I've made it a little better, but this is absolutely the best I can make it."

Kissinger replied, "Well, if that is the best you can make it, then I'll read it."

Give whatever you are doing your all. Become a living example of a class act. Become a person your son would want to follow. Just like you can teach your son many great habits with just a few seconds of work per day, you to can transform *yourself* into the picture of excellence with a little effort. It takes so little to rise above the mob. Do it!

CHAPTER 13
You've Got an Attitude . . .

We wear the mask that grins and lies.
                    —*Paul Laurence Dunbar*

A parents' most frequent complaint is about their son's bad attitude. This presenting complaint of "bad attitudes" isn't the real problem. The *real* problem is the disillusionment parents feel because the best effort they've put forward has been ineffective in changing their son. They lash out in frustration blaming "attitude problems" for their inadequacy. We need to banish this type of misplaced blame and give parents the knack for changing their sons!

The Two Species

These core attitudes form your basic orientation to life. If you were a computer, these would be called your "defaults" the orientations you always return to. These can run the range from optimistic, energetic, feisty, light-hearted and scrappy to deeply brooding, discontent, introverted, morose, overly tolerant and the like. Given their subtle nature, they hide well within the framework of a personality. They are difficult and time consuming to change.

The second species are *"Transient Attitudes."* These are attitudinal phases that come and go rapidly. Their cycle can be from seconds to days, and can emerge in many forms. These attitudes are the noticeable ones; joy, playfulness, excited, distractible, "blue," talkative, contrary, fickle, indecisive, self-pitying, depressed and so on. These are also the ones that draw most of the ire and disaffection of parents. They're also the easiest to change.

Attitudes Don't Always Operate Logically

Trying to investigate attitudes can be maddening work. At times it's like trying to understand the "thinking" of tornadoes! Attitudes are utterly capricious. Trying to use logic to understand them is futile. Illogic bewilders logic.

What controls attitudes? Perhaps biochemistry. Maybe they come and go due to spiritual causes. Perhaps an undiscovered level of mental/emotional function? These are questions open to speculation.

I wouldn't spend much time trying to unravel the knot. Trying to sort attitudes by understanding them can be like pouring slow acting acid on your resolve; you only end up scalding your attitude! It's natural to search for root causes and motives, but it's like catching fog . . . interesting but frustrating.

Forget the reason and cause for attitudes. They don't essentially matter in changing the order of things. What matters is having the optimism and method to change them if they are unacceptable to you or to your family.

African American Young Men Are Conscious of Their Attitudes

African American young men, especially the younger ones are cold blooded with respect to their attitudes.

Yes, you can influence attitudes in the mean time, and yes you should talk to your son about the situation. Don't expect him to understand, though. If you will recall our lessons from chapter 3, if you can't see, feel, touch, taste or smell it, it won't reckon in his head. Still, it always makes sense to try, for it's a mystery, what might connect.

Attitudes Are Prime Motivators

Motivation: We talk about motivation like we might know what it is, but really, we are still uncertain what makes people get up and go?

Each person seems to have their own idiosyncratic formula for thinking. *Attitudes* are the bowl that we use to we mix the basic ingredients. Without attitudes not much motivation happens. Prevailing moods and perspective can create a possibility for action.

That is why I call attitudes "prime motivators." Without the basic structure of proper attitude, getting even the most capable person motivated to act is practically impossible. Conversely, with the right structure the most talentless person can do the impossible.

"African American young men sculpting" is fun. This whole approach to building attitudes is based on the observation that specific body postures get connected over time to specific feelings and attitudes. When people are depressed, they tend to slump and slouch, walk slowly and have droopy faces. People that are happy walk erectly, with a quicker gate, and have a more "open" congenial look. Each of us develops very early in life specific postures for each specific attitude we experience.

That's what makes it possible for you to look at others and almost feel what they feel. That's what makes you so "readable" to others. Posture, gait, and emotion are "written all over you." An astute observer can easily perceive your condition. Go out in public and attune your senses to "how someone must be feeling to walk that way." Just practice this as you drive around. You'll become skillful, at guessing who's happy and who's grumpy.

You can change a young man's internal atmosphere by changing his external posturing. If for whatever reason your son is in some attitudinal orbit that you want him out of, make him change his posture, shift the way he sits, alter the speed with which he walks and talks, comb his hair, crosses his eyes, puts on ear rings, or anything! Just change some external parameter. Like the example of the links in a chain, alter one link, and the whole chain must readjust.

When you recognize an attitude that you realize your son needs, you must begin to magnify that attitude in *your* actions. Parents would be very disturbed to find out how little your sons can really describe about you. African American young men don't automatically pick up all your traits and values. You may very well have a trait about you that you feel is prominent and desirable, but your son does not even see it. What he sees may in reality, have little connection to what you think you show him.

This is very normal and explains why so many African American young men are so different from their parents. Perhaps these young men are blind or maybe you don't show yourself as clearly as you think you do. Either way, modeling requires that you focus, align and energize your attitudes along a direction that is unmistakably clear to your son.

This is accomplished by making your important attitudes more distinct. I would suggest that you limit your modeling to attitudes you really want your son to see. For example they might be, honesty, toughness, gentleness, diplomacy, forgiveness, aggressiveness and many others. Explain to him the value of these and demonstrate how as they arise from within you in real life situations.

He'll need to start spending some time with you for just watching. Your part is to make sure those attitudes spring from you *like you said they would*. If you have any doubt, get yourself together before you open your mouth. Your son will learn whatever you *show* for him, so be sure you know what it is, that you want to show him.

Here's your rule of thumb: When someone asks your son what you are like, make sure he has at least *three* things he can say about you. Could he do that today? Be distinctive. Make your opinions and attitudes impressive him deeply.

⧈ CHAPTER 14
Sports

Don't look back. Something may be gaining on you.

—Satchel Paige

I'm frequently asked about the "pressure problem" of kids sports. I'm going to give you a simple answer. Unfortunately, African American young men get slam-dunked into legitimate high pressure situations too early, causing bad reactions and well justified concern among parents. These influences require a down-to-earth and forthright action from you.

Pressure is inherent in everything we do. Whether at work, or at school, Church or at home, pressure comes from expectation, and the demand we feel to live up to our own and others' hope. Sports, by virtue of an audience, showcase these expectations and jack-up the pressure to a crushing level.

That pressure can be good or bad, depending on the source. There are two sources of pressure in sporting events: You, and the game. The pressures of the game are good, normal, and something all young men need to face. *The pressure from you is highly volatile, and must be handled delicately.* I don't know if you are one of these high pressure parents that wants your kid to win everything in sight, or one of the "couldn't-care-less" ones. You both exert your own style of pressure whether you are aware of it or not, and thus must apply the following antidotes to yourself.

Liberally apply patience and confidence to yourself and be patient with your kid! He will come along much faster and happier, if he knows he can count on you to calmly support him, quietly encourage his participation, and slowly help him build his own level of skill. You only end up shooting both of you in the feet, if you are full of bombast and "turn the screws down" to get performance. Approximately 10 percent of *young men* respond to this kind of pressure and get better. The other 90 percent respond to it by getting worse! Remember, African American young men are not adults, and what works to get performance out of adults has a different effect with your son.

You must bring confidence to the "pressure party." Your belief in your son is a virulent force. No matter what that kid does, no matter how he plays, you must tell him that you believe in him and believe he's the greatest person you have ever seen . . . and he can get even better! Proclaim your confidence in *him*, not in his athletics. You will turn that boy into a pressure master if you follow this advice.

Handling Pain

This is real life stuff! Blood and pain are a part of life, and in this age, sports are one of the few activities left that let African American young men safely rub up against the harsher side of reality. Our parental inclination is to shield our sons from this, but hard as it is, we must get out of the way and let it happen.

Young men scream and cry at pain for fear that it will never stop. To the mind of a child, that is how pain registers. It is only through experience that we all learn that pain will end, and that bumps, bruises and blood don't mean death.

This realization will come slowly, especially in our neighborhood. We see physical harm and danger that it takes children years to cope with. It is the cause for many children dropping out of sports programs prematurely. My advice is to overlook and discourage the "touchies." Don't let him become a slave to small hurts.

Thankfully sports allow us a way to teach harsher truths of life in a controlled way. Encourage your son to accept that bumps, bruises, and blood from sport activities are all right. He won't die. Teach him that just because he hurts doesn't mean he stops all together. Teach him that his body will work well even when it gets hurt, and to a *small* extent, he should press himself.

Losers are the ones with real opportunity in a sports match. They have the opportunity to look at what they did, and the chance to improve. If they handle a loss this way, they can look at themselves in the mirror and know they did their best in spite of losing. *They are the real winners.* Losers just lose and feel bad. Winners who simply gloat over victory are also losers. Only those who continually improve, win or lose, are fit to wear the garland of the champion.

The problem for you as a parent will be to communicate this to your son after a defeat! In older African American young men, the only pain I would suggest *encouraging* is the pain of not having done your "best." The pain of a loss in kids is usually a "dead-end pain"; it just hurts and doesn't move anywhere. Move your child off that pain and toward a focus of realistically assessing what they could have done better.

Athletic Extremes

There may be those among you, who for whatever reason, feel as though the treatment in the last chapter is *not* relevant for your son. Perhaps your African American young man is a legitimate athletic prodigy, and you have taken unusual steps to develop his athleticism on your own. Any discussion of sports you feel, may, be below the skyrocketing talent and potential of your son. If this is your situation, Godspeed to you! I wish you well.

There are probably many more parents who have African American young men who are possessed of little or no athletic skill. As much as you might wish or dream, the kid just hasn't got it. To add insult to injury, our sports crazy world might have driven your son to feel inadequate about his lack of talent, thereby making sports participation a hated struggle.

As a black culture, we have a strong bias toward the athletically chosen.

I'd like to make a suggestions to both the parents of the athletically gifted, and those of the athletically deprived. I feel compelled to reiterate to you that sports have less to do with athletics than with achievement. Athletics is simply another way to push yourself to "Be your Best." It may not even be the best way to achieve excellence, just one of the ways. This perspective has heavy implications for parents of both great athletes and non-athletes.

He's Good

True athletic genius, like other aspects of genius, is present at birth.

Unlike other fields of genius, athletes don't begin to "separate from the pack" until the middle of the African young man phase, around the age of eight to ten. Of course up until that time, he's been head and shoulders above the rest athletically, but *real active talent needs physical maturity to support ability.* This is also the time that a child prodigy begins to settle on a sport, or physical activity to make their mark.

Keep a close eye on the **pressure** you apply. Just like stress, there is a fine line separating pressure that is helpful, from pressure that is harmful. Throughout the young man phase, the pressure you apply should be focused more upon developing skill, than winning. There is plenty of time to win, but not much time to prepare the skills required for winning.

Get him a good **coach**. It can be anybody. African American young men simply respond better athletically to good coaches than parents. I realize that if your son wants to pursue an unusual sport like figure skating or gymnastics, you might feel the need to send him hours away for the best coach. Do that if you like, but frankly any reputable coach who stresses the basics will suffice at this age level. Whatever your son likes to do athletically, put him in with someone who possesses specialized knowledge. They can push your son's talent past the point that you can.

Teach him that there is more to life than "winning" (beating those of clearly lesser talent.) Athletic prodigies win all the time, and rarely have had the experience of losing. Winning "all the time" changes the lesson of head-to-head competition from "being your best" to "drubbing the opponent." This isn't good. Improving and achieving should be the focus, not simply testing an opponent.

I heard a touching story once about the Special Olympics. This is the Olympics for handicapped children. The hundred yard dash was hyped as the big event for the day. All the participants were waiting anxiously for the start. The official gun went off, and the crowd rose to their feet to see a smooth and fast beginning. All the racers were moving along as fast as they could when suddenly, one of the competitors in the center lane twisted his ankle and fell down on the track, squealing in pain.

The "usual" thing did not happen. One by one, the other competitors slowed down to look back and find out what had happened. Eventually, they all stopped running. In a most uncompetitive gesture, all the racers came to the aid of their stricken friend, helped him to his feet, *and carried him forward across the finish line!*

All of them became winners!

Help your son become well rounded. I've worked with many kids I've felt very sorry for. They had no social time, no opportunity to expand horizons, and no real variety in their life. Many of these athletic prodigies will end up pitifully naive about anything other than their sport. I don't like to see this happen. Don't let this happen to your son. No matter how talented he may be, give him some room to *vary*.

Lastly, teach your son to appreciate his natural gift and help those who are less fortunate. Natural genius of any sort is a gift, and not to be taken lightly. Keep your son humble, for he actually did nothing to earn his great skill. If he aspires to achieve great things with his talent, *then* he becomes something special. Encourage him to have some depth to his character by helping those less fortunate, teaching, and encouraging others how they too can become better. Outside of the entertainment value of watching the skill and grace of an athletic genius, it's the only way I know that an athlete can give back a little of what they've been given.

No Athlete

If your son cannot perform in one of the "Big Four" sports (football, baseball, basketball or soccer) he's dubbed an athletic geek. All boys who are pigeon holed in this fashion are painfully aware of their inadequacy. They are constantly reminded by the taunting of other young men, getting picked last for school yard games, and in gym class where they know they are complete misfits. Sports is a tough arena for the talentless. There are few places to hide.

I would make a number of suggestions to you. First, outside the physically handicapped, there are very few African American young men with *zero* athletic talent. Of the hundreds of organized sports in the world, there is a least one where your son could feel the joy of proficiency, and competitiveness with others. Think of the unusual like swimming, dancing, badminton, karate, archery, bicycle racing, track and field events, or scuba diving. Please don't consider your son athletically hopeless until you have explored a breadth of new options for physical competition.

Secondly, just as athletic genius requires physical maturity to be fully displayed, physical maturity will deliver hope to the talentless. Just because your son may lack any hint of skill today, does not mean that in six-months he might not have become more skilled with hand-eye coordination, improved balance, quickness and agility.

As a head football coach, I've witnessed terrific improvement in performance from year–to–year for no other reason than physical maturity.

The rates at which African American young man mature physically will vary widely as do the skills that accompany those changes. That should be a great relief to you and your son. Time works a strange magic for your son and he may suddenly become athletically competent for no apparent reason.

Thirdly, you will likely need to deal with the emotional consequences of peer mistreatment. Being ostracized by friends due to lack of athletic ability is agony for a kid. School gym classes attempt to reduce the chance of this by blending boys and girls, and requiring only simple athletic chores. Still, your son may have a defeating experience and feel very bad.

Consider this: Athletic play is the most important social ritual for African American young men, so help your son find other ways to fit in. Remember that being unable to participate in a specific sport or game *is not the kiss of social death!* Like dealing with young men who have physical handicaps, you must encourage him to be *as active as he is able*, and not to judge personal worth on the number of runs scored, baskets made or goals saved.

If all else fails, forget sports! It would be best if your son could be involved in some sport, but if this is not a reality, find another arena to stress achievement. Remember, *that's* the goal anyway.

This may in all candor leave you feeling disappointed, especially if you're a sports nut. You might have had fantasies of your son playing on toward some wonderful athletic achievement like a Heisman Trophy or an NBA championship. Those images might need to be shelved. I guess you'll

just have to play with some pain! Offset athletic disappoint-
ment and frustration in your son by helping him select
another area in which to excel.

Lastly, encourage your son to be vigorous. I have found
that what makes a difference in making your son fit socially,
is not so much his athletic talent, but the extent to which
your son can be excited and vigorous. This is not a physical
dimension, but an attitudinal dimension. Help your son to
thrive in any arena, irrespective of how well he thinks he
can do. Being excited and vigorous are the prime keys to
helping non-athletic African American young man succeed
and fit into a world that is heavily biased towards the athletic
elite.

⧉ CHAPTER 15
Self-Esteem

*A man who won't die for something is not fit to
live.*

—Martin Luther King, Jr.

"Self-esteem" is unfortunately becoming a shopworn echo in our lives. I feel a strong urge to share my discontent with this phrase, for like so many before it, the term has gained a life of its own and its' meaning has drifted far from the original. The fundamental concept is still good, but the common meaning is exhausted.

Colloquially it's defined as feeling good about yourself. Self-esteem was originally labeled in the fifties and sixties by Dr. Norman Vincent Peale, as feeling good about yourself based upon, accomplishments and skills, learned on the road to excellence. It means something very different today.

Now, building self-esteem through positive"self-talk," incessant praise and reward rate as the current psychological fix of choice for a wide array of behavioral dysfunctions! Examples of this self-talk are:

"I'm a good and deserving person"
"I'm a winner"
"I'm competent and growing stronger daily"
"I'm a good student and deserve the best"

Look, their is nothing wrong with saying good things to yourself. But, this constant self-praise has become epidemically foolish. We're encouraged to dole out praise to ourselves, and our children without plan or justification. It's like emotional welfare. If you breathe you deserve to be told you're wonderful. Our society has thrown around this self-praise stuff so often that it no longer means anything. It's no wonder people aren't tangibly improving. The incessant positive self-talk is without value!

The fact is, we all know deep down that we're not so great, and that excellence must be achieved. This is difficult to admit. We are notoriously prone to believe information that supports our most cherished hope about ourselves, *even when that information is idiotic or wrong*. The popular mental health doctrine holds that feeling good about yourself is the same as being good. This is an unfortunate ruse that only postpones the bitter truth that excellence must be earned.

If You Don't Believe in Your Son, You Are His Worst Enemy!

You must be relentless in your belief of your son. He knows very well if you believe in him, and if by chance he's unclear, he'll guess pessimistically. You must discipline yourself to speak forth boldly for your son, and confidently attack those areas he chooses to master. Hand-wringing and second-guessing are strictly forbidden! Your son needs to understand the plain fact that no matter what, you believe that he can do anything he sets his mind to and fully support his earnest efforts.

Brag about your son in front of other adults. What a great reward! What a vivid message! He will not only hear the words that you tell another adult with the ears of his heart he will hear that you love him and are proud to be his parent. That alone is worth the effort, to seek and, to brag to another person in front of your son.

You need to teach your son to disregard people when they say "no, it can't be done that way," or "you'll never be able to do that," or worse yet, "they won't let a Black man do that and you won't be able to either." Your son needs to master the skill of defiantly ignoring these bad mouth people.

Some of those people might be his best friends. The unfortunate truth is that friends are, often the biggest impediment to success. Unless a friend has the humility and love to help another up and out of the crawdad bucket, they are a phony replication of a real friend. Our lives are too valuable for anchors disguised as friends to hold us down.

Prepare to Ignore Bad Circumstances

It's possible to ignore the obstacles that life plants in your path. Some people just have a capacity to act as if problems don't exist, and plow forward. I do know that from the smallest feat, to the most awesome achievement, trouble will stalk you and impede the route. Will your son ignore them?

How should we teach African American young men about these problems? Well, because negative circumstances are always going to be there, I suggest that you prepare your son in advance, and let him know that trouble, discouragement and hardship are part of winning. A young man who knows that these are a part of the program, is not nearly as staggered as those, who get surprised by unanticipated difficulty.

Speak boldly to your son about the real life obstacles! Warn him! Suggest to him that he won't encounter anything that has not been faced before by other African American young men. Assure him of his talent and skill, and focus his attention on those, rather than the obstacles that may (or may not) lurk in the future.

You might even step further by showing him how to find the good in bad situations.

By all means, acknowledge any fears he may have, and urge him to try in spite of them. There is no finer way to pierce the nerve center of defeat than to forge ahead in spite of fear!

Reward with Attention

You must sharpen yourself to notice the efforts of your son as he attempts to master something. Challenge yourself to notice any initiative shown by your son and reward it with his favorite treat - your attention! Any "initiative" means any action he starts by himself for the purpose of learning or doing something new. This is a golden moment that comes more often than you think!

In fact, it might come your way daily. Our kids bring home school work everyday, and display it with considerable pride about all the work they've done. They don't do this routine for fun, they want us to be proud. I oblige that hunger by gushing all over them! Seize these brief moments without thinking, jump in and fan the fire! Take the time to show him you care.

I can hear many of you saying you wouldn't have the time available for this. Listen, your time is the greatest reward, you can give your son. Make time. If you haven't the luxury of much spare time in the day, I suggest a "time slot" to create more.

Help Find Some Good Heroes

Helping your son find good heroes must also be a high priority for you as a parent. Tell him stories of heroism, in African American history, introduce him to his past, his culture, and the people who have done wonderful things. Go out of your way to expose him to black history. I would suggest that you assume the responsibility for exposing your African American young man to our people of integrity and skill, letting nature take its course.

African American young men need heroes. Young men, due to the immature quality of their personality, are constantly on the hunt for adults to follow and emulate. That is part of how they naturally grow and develop. Who they choose for a hero is not always in your control, but your direction and advice are important determining factors.

Who do your African American young men most often choose for heroes? Black athletes, musicians and movie stars. You might want to keep in mind that a large part of the advertising hype for stars is aimed at developing a heroic public image. Advertisers understand the impact of heroes, and use this knowledge to sell more tennis shoes and sugar water. As we've watched countless public heroes stumble, it should be obvious that those we're told are heroes don't necessarily qualify.

Press the idea of selecting qualified and proven heroes with your son. Ask him some questions. Why does he like them? Specifically? What does he think that hero or role model could teach him if he had some time to spend with him? What valuable lesson can you, as dad or mom, learn from *his* heroes? What do his heroes tell you about his wishes, hopes, and dreams? If his hero was in his shoes, how would be conduct himself?

Don't try to railroad him into getting new heroes; just get him to think a bit about this whole business. Keep in mind that the purpose of a hero is to *set the pace for personal achievement*, not to have a new idol to worship. Help your son stop worshipping and start keeping pace with those he idolizes.

Getting Your Son to Do the Things
He Doesn't Think He Can

It is easy to get kids to do things they don't think they can do. Any talent consists of a combination of smaller actions that anyone can do. Climbing trees is grabbing one branch and pulling yourself up. Then, grabbing another branch and going up again. Playing a viola begins with picking up the instrument, and holding it. Then, putting one finger on one string, and pulling the bow across that one string. Becoming a world renowned virtuoso will take just a little more practice! Skateboarding? Find a skateboard and stand on it. Just stand on it! Within 10 minutes that will get boring, so put one foot on the ground. Within ten minutes, that will get boring, so push a little bit . . . and so on.

The reason African American young men have trepidation is because they become intimidated by looking at an entire polished activity and thinking "there's no way!!" They see only the top of a tree, or playing Beethoven, or skating in the national championships. You can get a young man to do most anything if you show him that any activity is a specific, *boring* sequence of behaviors, that they may already know how to do! Once shown that at the core, everything is, quite basic, most young men will gather the courage to try anything.

All you can do is fail, right? And what happens then? You get up and try it again. Simple.

Resourcefulness

Having an attitude of resourcefulness can give you the best possible chance to creatively impact the world around you.

When resourcefulness meets a problem, it says, "How can I fix it?"
When resourcefulness meets a need, it says "How can I fill it?"
When resourcefulness meets a challenge, it says "How can I whip it?"

When resourcefulness meets insurmountable odds and overwhelming adversity, it says "There must be a way." If there is any possible way to fix this, I can find it too. The answer won't jump up into my lap, so I better go find it, or find someone to find it, or find someone to find someone to find it . . ."

Do you get the idea? Resourcefulness is probably best described as the *inability to quit* in the pursuit of what you want. To actively search all of the options and to create them if necessary. It's best built with real world problems, combined with tutoring (from you). Don't permit your son to give up on the solution to a difficulty without exhausting all the avenues of answers.

Let's Win

We have fought on every battleground in America for our God-given rights. As our country is moving toward a global economy, we are still creeping toward gaining our rights. African American young men have seen hate-filled policemen curse, kick, brutalize and even kill their brothers and sisters. You find them trying to explain why they can't find a job, even after completing school. You see your son's personality developing a bitterness for the angry white people; you are humiliated day in and day out by discrimination; your first name becomes "nigger" and your middle name becomes "boy." Your wife and mother are never given respect. Day by day, night by night, you are faced with the fact that you're an African American living in a white society. Never knowing what to expect next . . . forever feeling discrimination.

So many of our young men have been condemned/robbed of life. Condemned for being black. Condemned for misguided popular beliefs.

Before the Pilgrims landed at Plymouth, we were here. Before Jefferson wrote the words of the Declaration of Independence, we were here. Our foreparents labored without wages to build the masters' homes. We have continued to thrive and develop. Slavery could not stop us. The opposition we now face will not stop us. Drugs, crime, black on black violence, will not stop us. We have God on our side.

Recommended Readings

From Race to Hope, Crystal Kuykendall, National Educational Services, Bloomington, Indiana 1992.

Understanding an Afrocentric World View, Linda James Myers, Kendall/Hunt Publishing Company, 1993.

What's So Bad About Being Good?, Jack R. Christianson, Bukcraft, Inc. 1992.

PaPa My Father, Leo Buscaglia, Fawcett Columbine, New York, 1992.

School Desegregation: Enough Is Enough, Bill Moss, Danmo Publishing Co., 1992.

Fancy titles before your name
or how well you played the game,
God deals with both of you the same.
If you fall short in life, I am to blame
because I taught you how to aim.
If you win and find fortune and fame,
then I know my life will not be in vain. Raising
sons can be a struggle and pain.
But you know I love you both the same.

—Harvey Alston